EFFECTIVE
NEGOTIATING

THE SUNDAY TIMES
BUSINESS SKILLS SERIES

"excellent ... well worth reading"
Christopher Lorenz, the *Financial Times*

The Sunday Times Business Skills Series is an up-to-the-minute collection of books covering essential management topics in the three key areas of total quality management, personal skills and leadership skills.

Combining current management theory and practice with detailed case examples and practical advice, each book provides a definitive stand-alone summary of best management practice in a specific field. While each book is complete in itself, books in the series have been carefully co-ordinated to complement *The Sunday Times* Business Skills video training package of the same name produced by Taylor Made Films (see inside back flap for more details).

Books already published in the series:

PERFORMANCE APPRAISALS
Martin Fisher
ISBN 0 7494 1441 3

MANAGING CHANGE
Philip Sadler
ISBN 0 7494 1343 3

EFFECTIVE NEGOTIATING
Colin Robinson
ISBN 0 7494 1344 1

BUILDING YOUR TEAM
Rupert Eales-White
ISBN 0 7494 1342 5

ACHIEVING BS EN ISO 9000
Peter Jackson and David Ashton
ISBN 0 7494 1440 5

EFFECTIVE NEGOTIATING

Colin Robinson

KOGAN
PAGE

First published in 1995

Kogan Page Limited
120 Pentonville Road
London N1 9JN

British Library Cataloguing in Publication Data

A CIP record for this book is available from the British Library.

ISBN 0 7494 1344 1

Typeset by Saxon Graphics Ltd, Derby.
Printed in England by Clays Ltd, St Ives plc

Contents

Preface

It is inevitable in a book of this type that much of the content draws on personal experience. It must, therefore, reflect the background of the writer. But this should not be permitted to impose too many constraints on the reader and should not unduly limit the readership.

It may or may not be possible to discern my own background from what has been written. It has been in construction, manufacturing and distribution and, latterly, in management consulting, again with a flavour of the construction industry and its many users. In all the roles that I have played, negotiation of one sort and another has been prominent. Perhaps I have done more than my fair share and perhaps that has been because my colleagues have discerned that I have always enjoyed it. Those who enjoy something inevitably make more effort at it.

Throughout the book I use the term 'opponent' to describe the person or people against whom the negotiator is pitting himself. Although some people believe this suggests a confrontational attitude rather than a collaborative approach, I use it very much in the sporting sense.

In the late 1960s, as manufacturing industry – with other sectors following – began to expand the concept of partnership between suppliers and users of materials and components, negotiation took on greater significance to the longer-term strategy of the business and those who negotiated were often more senior than had been involved previously. But they were not always better negotiators, and certainly not better simply because they were more senior. Seniority brings extra authority to commit the business, it brings different experience, but neither guarantees that the person will be a better negotiator.

There are many examples of negotiation in the book, presented in a number of different forms. Some were supplied by colleagues, some by friends, others have been drawn from my own experience, a few have been created from my imagination to augment important messages, while some have been compiled from more than one such origin in order that they should fit the text and highlight something from it. My thanks are due to all of those who have supplied examples and who have told me of lessons learned and insights gained into the art and science of negotiation.

The illustrations have been drawn by my colleague at KPMG, Peter Langridge. It is difficult to decide who should prepare illustrations but Peter and I have worked together for some years and we suffer similar senses of humour. I am delighted at the way he has put his finger on the essence of what I have written and said it in pictures with greater clarity and brevity than it is said in words.

Throughout the production of the text, I have had very considerable support from KPMG, with whom I do my 'day job'. This has arisen not only in respect of having ready access to our sophisticated networked text processing system, but also with regard to colleagues' willingness to accept a modicum of shortness of temper on my part when the pressures were greatest.

Pauline Goodwin of Kogan Page invited me to write this book and gave the initial guidance about style, content and approach. In this she was reflecting the requirements of *The Sunday Times* and interpreting them into what she knew of my style and thoughts. Whilst she and her colleagues have set almost impossible deadlines, they have also provided excellent support to ensure that they have been achieved.

But, clearly, the family takes the major brunt of such a task. To them, thanks.

Colin Robinson
Harpenden
October 1994

1

Introduction

For fools rush in where angels fear to tread.

Alexander Pope, *An Essay on Criticism*.

You have picked up this book because you want to be a better negotiator.

Not, perhaps, because you think you might be a bad one at
present; nor, perhaps, because you want to start from the very
beginning, but because you recognise that there is always something
left to learn and that to 'fear to tread' is a wise approach.

Nobody starts from the very beginning in negotiation because we
can all negotiate something, somehow. We negotiate almost from
the day we are born. We cry when we want attention and if we
don't get it, we cry some more. Maybe in the very early stages we
do not quite do this as a deliberate negotiation, but we very soon
learn how to handle the crying bit to get just what we want. And
we also very soon learn that we might not get quite what we
wanted, but have to settle for second best.

So we *can* all negotiate. And this book contains much useful
information and guidance as to how to do it better.

But it is not only about becoming a better negotiator. The book
very deliberately follows the theme that you should enjoy negotiating. If you do not enjoy doing something, you will not do it quite
as well as you otherwise might. That is certainly true of negotiation.
Many of the chapters and pointers in this book should help you
relax and have greater confidence when negotiating and thus help
you derive both pleasure and satisfaction from the exercise.

In the many seminars and other sessions I have run on the art
and science of negotiating, I have always stressed this point about
enjoyment. Nothing is worse for your side than an individual or
team member who is frightened of being involved in negotiation,

worried about what he or she might give away, or uncertain as to what outcome might be satisfactory. That person will derive neither pleasure nor satisfaction at the end of the job and will find every reason for avoiding the task next time round.

Enjoyment, therefore is my central theme.

The Angry Golfer

'How did you get on in your match today?'

'Don't even ask. I was awful. I lost on the thirteenth. The thirteenth! Against him! The thirteenth. I nearly walked off after the ninth and gave it to him. I was so awful. I looked so stupid and useless. I can't go back to the club for months and face them. The thirteenth! It was ridiculous. Do you know, when we arrived to tee off at the sixth . . . Why do I try to play this game . . . The thirteenth . . . '

'Surely if you don't enjoy it you will never play well, and if you don't play well, you will never enjoy it. Why don't you leave the game to someone who does enjoy it and is better at it?'

'But the thirteenth . . .'

That enjoyment can be derived not only from the challenge of negotiating as part of a job and from the knowledge that a project has been completed well and to your advantage, but also in a personal sense. Good negotiators at work are also good negotiators in their personal lives. The good business negotiator will buy personal things better than others, will actually negotiate when others did not think to do so and will do consistently better deals in domestic circumstances than others. This applies to buying things cheaper, obtaining things that others thought were out of stock, and having work done at home at convenient times rather than when somebody else says it can be.

Negotiation, then, is about life, and life is about negotiation.

In many places in this book, the analogy between negotiating and sport is drawn. Except for those few people for whom playing sport has become so much a business that any enjoyment has disappeared, except for the enjoyment of making yet more money, there is little point in playing sport unless you enjoy it. If you do not gain pleasure and personal satisfaction from both negotiation and sport – even if both can at times be intensely frustrating – then let someone else do it.

WHY IS THIS BOOK DIFFERENT?

Why indeed is this book different from almost all the others on the market? There are three principal answers to this question.

○ First, it focuses on the elements of negotiation that arise well before you go into the room and sit opposite the opposing team.

○ Second, it sets out to offer real advice and guidance from which to draw in handling each of the critical stages of a negotiation, drawn from the real practical experience of a large number of people.

○ Third, throughout the book there are clearly identified sections which indicate the significance of what has been written to the person with responsibility for managing negotiators.

I have been encouraged to ensure emphasis on this first point by reaction to my previous book, in which much the same line was taken. Too many writers and teachers seem to be quite unaware of this point and suggest that you start negotiating when you arrive opposite your counterparts from the other side. That is nothing short of nonsense and this absolutely critical success factor will be examined in detail at a number of places in this book.

The second point is of great importance because so much on the subject of negotiation seems to be written by people who have never been there themselves. When I read many of the books currently available, and seemingly successful, I cringe at their naivety and the lack of accuracy that arises in many places. Just turn to their sections on how to negotiate with Russians/Japanese/Arabs and so on and then ask anyone who actually has negotiated with such people what they think of the advice. Ask and stand back!

But there is another aspect of my second point above which bears special attention. That is that the book does not set out to tell anyone how to negotiate. Instead, it sets out to provide a toolbox from which to take whatever you need to do any specific job. It also seeks to identify which tools might be best in different circumstances and to help readers ascertain just how and when each should be used.

> I find myself intolerant of management books that seek to prescribe exactly 'how it should be done'. My own experience shows that there are many different ways of achieving one's aims . . . Each one of us has to develop our own style, and our own approach, using such skills and personal qualities as we have inherited.
>
> What each of us does over a long period of trial and error is to acquire a set of tools with which we are comfortable and which we can apply in different ways to the myriad problems which we need to solve.
>
> (John Harvey-Jones, *Making it Happen – Reflections on Leadership*)

I hope John Harvey-Jones would not object to the fact that this book goes some way down the road of prescribing – in that it sets out the framework within which one should work – but does not then 'prescribe' too much within that framework. It is, therefore, a mixture of tools and prescription, but making every effort to maintain an appropriate balance.

Figure 1.1 illustrates the toolbox principle. There are many tools available to the trained negotiator, many of which appear superficially appropriate for any given negotiation. As the negotiation planning and preparation progresses, using the processes set out in this book, the focus will be increasingly on certain of the tools, while others will progressively be seen to have less relevance. When the whole of that particular matter has been dealt with, there will be seen to be a small number of tools that actually did most of the work and probably one that you would say truly opened the door and made sure the deal could be done in the way you were seeking.

The third point – that of carrying responsibility for the work of negotiators – is also important because the art of managing negotiators has much in common with general management thinking, but there are crucial additional points to be learned. Negotiators have to be given responsibility, they have to take risks, they have to work to uncertain outcomes, they have to back their own judgement and, on many occasions, they have to ride along with their hunches.

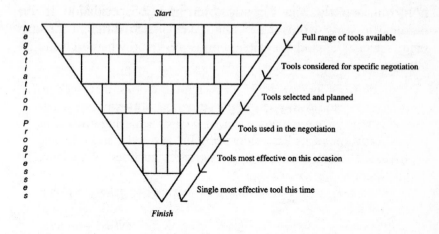

Figure 1.1 Selecting from the negotiator's toolkit.

Managing that sort of issue is clearly difficult. The aim here is, then, to offer some guidance as to how this may be done.

It is interesting to draw again on the sporting analogy in this respect. Coaching and basic training for sports tend to teach everybody to play to the same style and to use the same techniques. As one's game develops – whatever game it is – the good coach can identify how the player needs to strengthen in a specific area but not simply revert to one totally standard approach. The good coach will build on what is there, perhaps sometimes taking away a substantial chunk of bad practice and substituting something better which suits the player. Mainly, however, the good coach will identify the strengths of the player, build on them, make a few adjustments and enhance the overall standard. If the individual or the coach sees that the player seems to be bettered regularly in any particular aspect of their game, then that is the aspect on which to concentrate for the next few training sessions and matches.

We must do much the same thing with negotiators. This book does not seek to start the totally unaware down the path of negotiation but to take the player who has already been on court on a number of occasions, enjoyed the challenge, and who wishes from now on to learn to defeat even more able opposition. This book will hold out opportunities for improvement but it can only be the player who selects from the lessons, takes on board the aspects that seem attractive and possible, implements them and thereby improves.

THE PURPOSE OF THIS BOOK

...the simple plan
that they should take who have the power
and they should keep who can.

William Wordsworth, Rob Roy's Grave.

That sums up the purpose of negotiation. You should ensure that you have the power to take – of which more later – as well as the power to keep what you already have. During the negotiation you will attempt to argue your side's view while the other side argues theirs. No matter what you are negotiating, the whole point is to advance your own position and diminish that of the other side; otherwise, why are you doing it?

The extent to which you win will depend on a number of factors including:

O how good a negotiator you are and how good is the opposition;

O how well each of you has prepared;

O the cohesion of your respective teams;

O the time each of you has to pursue the issue;

O the real strength of each of your cases.

The aim of this book is to help you win more from negotiations. It will do that by addressing each of these issues as well as many other topics which lie on the levels below these headline factors. Although each will be dealt with in detail later, let us look briefly at these points here.

There are ways in which you can assess how good a negotiator you are – but you have to be honest with yourself and be willing to take both advice and criticism from others. You will not be able to assess accurately how good your opponent is unless you have some clear benchmarks against which to make your judgement. If those judgements are flawed because your baseline is inaccurate – that your interpretation of your own abilities is unreliable – then you will be taking wrong decisions about how to manage those particular negotiations. Throughout this book you will find pointers as to your own level of skill and be able to assess your strengths and weaknesses.

He that would govern others, first should be
The master of himself.

Philip Massinger, *The Bondman*.

"...very informal, Jim and I usually renew the contract over a cup of tea"

The topic of preparation is of critical importance in negotiation. It has long been a view among the most thorough and competent negotiators that they will win or lose a negotiation before they ever set foot across the threshold of the room in which they will meet the other side. Later chapters will return to this theme and address it in more detail. Suffice it to say at this point that there is a significant difference between the approach proposed in this book and that customarily taken elsewhere.

Too many writers and lecturers on this subject assume that the fun starts when you have entered the room to greet the opposing team. It does not – it started well before you arrived there. Unless you have armed yourself fully for this first meeting, you will lose. Some people may appear to be able to simply walk into a negotiation, command attention, pull off a brilliant deal and saunter out again. Most of us cannot do that, and those that think they can have probably caused far more disasters than they have had triumphs. And even if that person does pull off what seems to be a triumph based on no preparation whatsoever, look deeper and find out just what they have been doing recently. You may find a surprising amount of preparation.

Genius is one per cent inspiration and ninety-nine per cent perspiration.

Thomas Alva Edison, interview – *Life*, 1932.

In general, the more complex negotiations need to involve teams. Certainly it helps even on simpler tasks to have two heads rather than one but perhaps the organisation cannot afford to have double manning all the time on such things. In any event, poor team working can blow your efforts, so we will be looking at how to strengthen it and how to decide whether a team is needed, how to select it and how to manage it.

Now who will stand on either hand
And keep the bridge with me?

Thomas Babington Macauley, *Lays of Ancient Rome,* 'Horatius i'.

Even when you are to negotiate on your own, the question of the time available to carry out the full preparation will be difficult to resolve. There never is enough time to do everything that you would want to do because commercial pressures and those from colleagues will require you to get on with the negotiation. We have here, then, a matter of deciding just how much time would be justified in pursuing the preparation stage of a negotiation. There is no absolute answer to that; it is a matter of judgement.

Le mieux est l'ennemi du bien.
(The best is the enemy of the good.)

Voltaire, *Dictionnaire Philosophique.*

Of course, regardless of the amount of effort you put in to understanding yourself and the person or people who will be opposite you, to preparing, to building good and effective teamwork and to ensuring that optimum use is made of your team's time, a weak underlying case can still leave you without a win. But thorough work on all of these aspects can make your weak case stronger, the other side's apparently strong case weaker and your prospects of an outcome highly satisfactory to your side far more likely.

COVERAGE – WHAT SORT OF NEGOTIATIONS?

Many types of negotiation are heavily influenced by political and emotional factors and these may often outweigh the factual and objective elements. Further, the two sides in a negotiation may well see things with quite a different balance between the subjective and objective factors.

Now Do Let Us Be Reasonable

'Listen here, Smith, you are jolly well going to have to be sensible. Let the hostages go, throw out your weapons and come out with your hands up, old sport.'

'Clear off or I'll shoot everyone. You took my kid away from me. I'm going to get someone for that.'

'Now, now, Smith, old chap, no good can come of this. Why can't we discuss it like reasonable and civilised people? You can get treatment, you know, in a nice comfy place.'

'It's this lot that's going to need treatment. I want my kid back. I'm going to count to five...'

In hostage situations, many of the conventional issues dealt with in negotiation training may appear to become irrelevant as the emotional aspects take over and carry far greater weight. However, even in these circumstances, a great deal of commercial negotiation wisdom does still apply – you should still prepare thoroughly, for example, and you still have to know what it is you are seeking to achieve and to be able to see the issue from the other person's point of view. In the example, the negotiator is quite unable to see that he is augmenting the damage that has occurred already rather than helping the situation, and is increasing the breadth of the gap that the subsequent negotiation will have to bridge – hopefully with another negotiator being brought in before any serious injury is caused!

Certain hostage negotiations are good examples of two sides having quite different objectives and can involve very high degrees of emotion and irrationality. Others, however, for example where hostages are taken for hard, well-reasoned political or financial reasons, may have nothing to do with emotion and the negotiator who is trying to resolve such issues needs to recognise that injury to the hostages, or even killing them, may be used simply as another device for obtaining concessions. Such extremes require very specific training and there is no attempt to deal with it in these chapters.

Figure 1.2 shows that commercial negotiators can be successful while demonstrating both appreciably emotional traits and subjective judgement. What determines their success in any given circumstances is not whether they are susceptible to subjectivity or emotion but the extent to which these characteristics take over to the exclusion of objectivity and rationality. As with so many things in negotiating, it is a matter of balance and the circumstances.

It can be seen, then, that much of what is taught to commercial negotiators does apply to non-commercial situations. Whether one is handling a hostage issue, negotiating to be permitted to retain the right of veto in a European Union political forum, or trying to explain to your boss why his or her style prevents the department achieving its objectives, it pays to be well informed about the skills of commercial negotiation. These will then form the baseline from which the other skills may be developed – be they the specific psychology of hostage-takers, the obtuse logic of political deal-making, the development of inter-personal relationships, or many others.

So the information, guidance and advice available in this book will help all types of negotiator, but the content is aimed principally at those who seek to reach commercial understandings and arrangements.

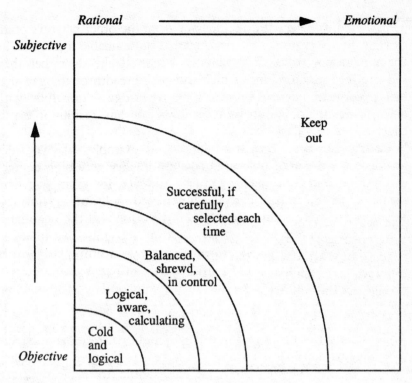

Figure 1.2 Balancing the extremes in negotiator selection.

PARTNERING

Nowadays in the field of commercial deals, much attention is focused on partnering, or developing long-term relationships. While this does represent something of a shift in thinking, perhaps leading to long-term contracts, joint ventures, cross ownership in each others' companies or open-book accounting, it also requires some adjustment to the processes involved in the negotiation. But it makes no real difference to the principles and the stages through which the negotiator should go. If one is aiming to set up a long-term relationship, it has to be based on trust with both parties seeing that the deal in is their long-term interests and that they do wish to be locked in for the period agreed.

Is this so different from the negotiation that goes on in every other aspect of business? It certainly should not be. There will be occasions when a negotiator drives the hardest bargain regardless of whether

BP Explores Partnering

For around four years, BP Exploration Europe has been developing and applying an innovative form of partnering, designed to deliver their major capital investment projects at lower cost, reflect an equitable sharing of risk between the client and contractors and provide an incentive to all to work cooperatively together. They call this 'Alliancing' and have used it on oil and gas exploration projects, where costs were expected to run into many millions of pounds.

Alliancing requires a fundamental shift in the relationships between BP and their contractors and between the contractors themselves. The aim is to reduce the combative nature of projects, whereby each contractor attempts to increase his own income at the expense of the client and the other contractors. BP identified that this adversarial approach was a damaging feature of many projects throughout the industry.

BP now operates an early competitive tendering process to select contractors, with only 50 per cent weighting being given to cost factors. Contractors' expertise is then available to the BP project team during the pre-sanction planning stage. Relying on considerable openness about costs and risks during the negotiation of contracts, a project cost is defined by the 'allies' and an agreement made about sharing any savings or overspends against that target. Arrangements are set out for dealing with totally unexpected occurrences and all involved can then see that cooperation, pooling of skills and delivery of a timely, top quality product is in everybody's interest.

The best way to highlight the advantages of this innovative form of partnering is to quote BP themselves, writing about development of the Hyde gas field:

In the event, the project was completed some 25 per cent below the agreed target cost. This result was not only highly satisfactory from BP's point of view but with the contractors taking a large share of the savings, their levels of profit were substantially above those they would normally expect.

Bob Scott
BP Exploration Technology Directorate
Competitive Advantage Through Alliancing
6th European Conference of the European Construction Institute
November 1994

> The same paper indicates that, on their Andrew field development, and starting from a base already some 20 per cent below their previous level of expectation:
>
> *...the alliancing approach is encouraging new levels of cooperation between all the parties leading to cost and time savings. For example the alliance has been able to find around £10 million of savings and to bring forward the projected completion date by two months.*

the other side really feels happy with the outcome – but if the other side agrees, why should the winner worry? The great majority of negotiations are not like that – we have to feel that when the written contract is sent off to be signed, it will be; we will not receive the response 'Sorry, but we have thought further about this and want to withdraw.' Whenever that occurs, everyone has lost out.

Certainly, in those partnering deals in which I have been involved, there has been very little real difference in the way each side handled itself from the approaches used in more run-of-the-mill once-off negotiations. We have assumed that the people on the other side were highly competent, knew their objectives, knew what they were prepared to accept and what they were not and would not lose sight of these factors during the negotiation. We have also assumed that they wanted the deal about as much as we did and would make significant efforts to be flexible enough to achieve it. We certainly did not feel any obligation to help them in their task, and they did not help us. In the end, with two competent teams pursuing some quite tough negotiations, some good and lasting deals were struck, and sometimes the parties agreed that there was not enough common ground to interest them and they parted. But in all the cases, the two teams were quite willing to consider negotiating subsequent deals with each other.

COLLABORATORS OR OPPONENTS?

In much of the writing and speaking that I do on the subject of negotiating, covering both partnership deals and shorter-term once-off contracts, I often use the word 'opponent' to describe the person or people against whom the negotiator is pitting himself. Although there are those who believe that this immediately sets up an attitude of confrontation, rather than a collaborative approach that seeks out acceptable outcomes in a spirit of cooperation and mutual support, I prefer to think of the people whom I am up against as opponents in the sporting sense. For me, the word retains the balance between the concept of winning and of walking off the court or pitch still able to talk to the other side, but not quite to the point of my team and our opponents sharing the changing-room bath – we must keep some team spirit and rivalry alive. Just how much rivalry in any given circumstances has to be left for you to judge.

"It may be a rugby tradition but I don't want you swapping tops with the chief buyer again"

Rugby Tour in South Africa

But the EPRU (Eastern Province Rugby Union) took no action against Elandre van den Berg for the stamping which opened up Jonathan Callard's face and needed 25 stitches. Instead it expressed outrage against England for purporting to be innocents in the battle... Trevor Jennings, the union's president, even suggested it was all a vicious English pre-test plot...'We think it is all part of England's psychological warfare to intimidate both players and referees as part of the build-up to the Test match.'

(Steve Bale, *The Independent*, 10 June 1994.)

In the context of sport, opponents are the people against whom you are competing and whom you intend to better in the competition. Just because they are opponents does not mean you have to hate them, or try to defeat them utterly, or grind them into the dust. The essential point is that there is a contest that you intend to win and you should never take your eye off that objective. Similarly with negotiation. The whole purpose of negotiating is to gain more for your own side than you have already and to leave less for the other side. Why bother otherwise?

The book often uses sporting analogies to examine the practice of negotiation against a number of types of opponent. These may be from other business entities with whom you wish to do short- or long-term deals, representatives of employee or management groups against whom you have to represent your faction's interests, and your colleagues. In situations where you are negotiating with colleagues, they become the opposition just as much as do buyers, vendors or others with whom you would reach agreement and do business.

ARE NEGOTIATORS BORN OR BRED?

But be not afraid of greatness; some men are born great, some achieve greatness, and some have greatness thrust upon them.

William Shakespeare, *Twelfth Night*.

We can readily substitute the concept of a good negotiator for that of greatness in this quotation. Some people certainly do seem to have been born with very considerable skills as negotiators – they seem to be 'naturals'. But just like kings and queens, they can benefit from clear specific training in their life's work as well as from on-the-job experience. Even though they start good, they then improve as they go along. On the other hand, where people do not have this strength of natural talent that leads them to be highly competent and natural negotiators, the talents with which they were born can be brought out and developed to enable them to reach a very high level of competence. That, in fact, is the position in which the great majority of us find ourselves; we have some talents for the various things we have to take on and have to improve with training and practice.

Where people have a requirement to negotiate 'thrust upon them', things become a little more worrying. Without the natural talent, without appropriate training, without the relevant learning experiences, they may well lead their organisations into deals which really should never have been countenanced. That is the fault of the person who did the thrusting, a person who cannot be considered either a competent manager in this respect or a competent negotiator in his own right.

The conclusion must be that we can all improve from whatever base we started and become better negotiators. As with the sporting analogy used elsewhere, some will become champions, others will become good at what they do and find their level of competition, but everyone can take part at some level or another and all should be able to enjoy their participation.

ARE FOREIGNERS REALLY ALL THE SAME?

Although there are a few examples of negotiations which have been held with foreigners dotted through the book, it will be noted that there is no attempt to define rules for negotiating with one nationality or another. We all recognise that when we negotiate with people with whom we are familiar and with whose company we feel to be natural, we see them as individuals and assess them, their skills, their techniques and their power as negotiators. We judge each not by set rules that we had clearly in our heads before we started, but by using good sense and the training we have had as negotiators.

Why then, when we start to think about negotiating with specific nationalities – say Russians, Germans or Chinese – do we seek simple rules and try to convince ourselves that they tell us all we need to know and which seem to override both common sense and our training? In what you read here, you will find that we do not fall into that trap as many other writers do. There are two reasons for this.

O *First*, in negotiating with Arabs, Belgians, Americans, Russians, the French and so forth, I have discovered that there are no golden rules. Each of my opponents – for opponents they have always been in my eyes – has been different and most of them have been as different from their stereotype as I hope I am from the stereotypical Englishman. In other words, ny own experience has demonstrated the utter folly of writing chapters headed 'How to negotiate with . . . (insert here the nationality of your choice)'.

O *Second*, from time to time, I still become involved in such negotiations in a number of countries on my own behalf, with colleagues and with clients. I would not dream of letting them see that I had already made so many erroneous judgements that it would be wiser if I was dropped from the team.

Here you will not read about national stereotypes. The entire book requires you to make judgements in your negotiating and not start from fixed points which will in the majority of cases be found to serve you quite badly.

STANDARD MANAGEMENT TEXTS

A great deal could be written about negotiation that would reflect exactly the wording of the standard texts on management. This is because negotiation is a sub-set of management more generally. Most management books will, for example, have extensive sections covering such features as:

O Leading
O Planning
O Coaching
O Delegating
O Monitoring
O Appraising
O Controlling

What they cover is directly relevant to negotiation but the general management aspects will not be repeated here. The approaches, techniques and methods of analysis which are dealt with in this book are to be read directly alongside texts on general management wisdom and neither supersede nor contradict them. The two sets of skills need to be understood and practised in parallel. This does not make the game impossible to learn or unduly complex to play, but it does make it far more challenging!

Before leaving this introduction to the book and what it has to say about the art and science of negotiation:

○ If you are hoping to find out how to negotiate the release of hostages, read on. You will find much useful material, but will certainly need further specific training.

○ If you are hoping to discover how to become the next Prime Minister, please also read on. This book may be the key factor in saving the nation billions of pounds.

○ If you are intending to confront your boss with his failings, you would also be well advised to read on. This book may help you keep your job and perhaps even get his.

And, of course, if you wish to improve your skills in the commercial field, be it in respect of buying or selling, personnel matters or reaching agreement with colleagues or business contacts, and whether you are seeking one-off deals or longer-term relationships, then you should certainly read on. It is for you that this book has primarily been written.

2

Know yourself, your colleagues and the opposition

Know then thyself, presume not God to scan,
The proper study of mankind is man.

Alexander Pope, An Essay on Man.

In this chapter we will examine some of the personal factors to be taken into account when negotiating. They will be addressed at this stage in general terms but will then be referred to at different points in the text and be related to the specific circumstances that can arise during each of the stages of a negotiation. At the end of the chapter, we look at an approach that can help you assess your own driving forces – the things that tend to make you behave and respond in the way that you do.

This is useful in enabling you to assess how these driving forces may be significant in any particular negotiation, and to see how those ranged against you may have an impact on the outcome of your joint activities. When team negotiations are discussed, you may also wish to consider how these driving forces impact on the interplay between team members and how they can be used for the good of the team.

It is important that you have a realistic idea of your own strengths and weaknesses in relation to negotiation. Not only so that you can be as effective as possible in applying the skills you have but also so that you can have them topped up as needed, by receiving coaching or specific training, according to the needs of the time. Having such knowledge and awareness gives you the opportunity to strengthen the weaknesses, to try different techniques relating to both your strengths and weaknesses and to focus on your strengths when facing your opponent. Knowing yourself is the first necessity of a good negotiator.

No man is demolished but by himself.

Thomas Bentley, A Letter to Mr Pope.

INTROVERTS AND EXTROVERTS

I have never come across a true introvert who was a good negotiator. Good, that is, at every stage of the process from inception to completion. The good negotiator has to be something of an actor, has to take chances from time to time, and has to be able to relate easily to the other side and to the team of which he or she is a member. Not only that but the good leader of a team of negotiators and the good solo negotiator has eventually to face the opponents and make the agreements. The negotiator who is not willing to accept the responsibility for at least some of the more significant aspects of the deal will not be seen by opponents as real but only as a mouthpiece.

This does not imply that more introverted types cannot contribute, and contribute significantly, to the negotiating process. They may excel at preparation, may develop strong, robust, flexible strategies, may evaluate outcomes and be able to provide powerful guidance to individuals or teams throughout the process. But they are unlikely to be the driving forces during the process itself.

But what of extroverts? Here we have a group that will tend to be stronger at dealing direct with opponents and may even race too quickly ahead in order to reach that stage – they enjoy it and want to get there without too much delay.

Audentis fortuna iuvat.
(Fortune favours the brave.)

Virgil, Aeneid.

Yes, these are generalisations. But they are made in order to focus attention on the different characteristics that arise and identify that any given negotiation will require a balance of skills. The more complex and protracted a negotiation, the more there is a need to bring in different skills from different people at different times. In simpler negotiations it may not be possible or economically sensible to involve too many people and the choice has to be made as to which of those available has the best balance of skill in that particular instance.

Let Me Get At Them

One of my colleagues at KPMG has a very alert mind and is much sought after to assist clients in developing forward-looking business strategies that challenge their own long-held views and assumptions about their industries.

When we have the opportunity to visit a potential client to discuss how we might help them, she will immediately dive into the discussion of options, their attitudes, the problems inherent in the business frameworks within which they operate and their customers' perceptions. Given her head, she would then go straight ahead with whatever work she perceived as needed, her energy, interest and competence becoming quite apparent to the client.

I usually go along with her for this first visit. Someone has to be there to keep our feet on the ground and ensure that costs, terms of reference, timescales, deliverables and relationships are debated and concluded so that both the client and we know how we will be operating and, at the end, whether we have done what we set out to do.

Of course, I am often involved in the work itself but I have no doubt and no illusions that it is clear to the client where the excitement and inspiration in the job is coming from. Then towards the end of the engagement, someone has to review what has been done and look over the final presentation to see that the client will get what was expected and what has been paid for.

We work together well as a team. We both have skills to bring. We could both do certain types of work in this area without the other. When the tricky ones come along it is clear that the synergy that can be developed requires us to hit the job together. Everybody benefits.

"We might be in trouble Sir, they have sent their extrovert team to negotiate"

INHIBITIONS

Just as it is possible to identify that true introverts tend not to make the best negotiators, so it is with people who are inhibited in particular ways. This may be considered as another feature of introversion, but is worth examining separately from that topic.

During a negotiation, it is essential to question, to challenge, to seek clarification and even to exhibit disbelief at what you are being told. Without this, you will be unable to examine the other side's case in sufficient depth or to obtain the amount of information you may require to make truly informed comparisons with other opponents' offerings and to reach correct decisions. Seeking such elucidation is a normal part of the negotiation process, often made difficult by someone who wishes to obfuscate certain factors. The negotiator who is unwilling to appear disbelieving or unconvinced by the data made available by that point in the discourse will not succeed.

On similar lines, one has to be willing to walk away from a deal that is not acceptable and which will not become acceptable. It does take a certain courage to say at a point, after you and your opponent have spent considerable time and effort to make the progress you have, that you see no point in carrying on. Such an approach is a useful trick that may obtain further concessions but, if you say that the deal is off and nothing more is offered, you have to mean it or lose credibility. The ability to walk away has to be developed and there are methods of preparation which can support the negotiator in this – these are discussed in a later chapter.

STATUS – REAL AND APPARENT

You will not be able to negotiate successfully unless your negotiating counterpart perceives that you have the status and authority to do so. There would be no point in even starting if there was a feeling that you could not commit to the matters you were discussing as, in such an event, your opponent would be giving information, offering exchanges of concessions and trying to trade off different aspects while you were simply listening, offering, proposing and then returning subsequently to say that nothing you had signalled was to stand. Your opponent must, therefore, have the confidence that you *do* have appropriate status and that negotiating with you is for real.

But do you actually have to have the authority which is perceived? No, not for the first negotiation – for that you can pretend and sustain the pretence for some time. When eventually the truth becomes clear, you no longer have any credibility in any negotiation, even one for which you do have appropriate standing. Then you must pass over for other negotiators to deal with that particular opponent, who may well choose not to believe that they have authority either.

There will certainly be occasions when you may have to overstep the limit of your responsibility during a negotiation but you have to ensure quite quickly afterwards that you gain approval for what has been done or return to the other side and retract. While retraction will undermine your standing and create circumstances where you have to bring another – more senior – person in on the more significant aspects of the deal, you will at least be seen by your opponent to be dealing in a straightforward way and to be open about your limitations.

At times, working near to the limits of your negotiating authority can resemble the actions of a swan. The swan, serene, calm, regal, in control and able to move as and where it wishes in a quite effortless way, is, in fact, paddling like mad beneath the surface. Just so the negotiator at or beyond the limits of delegated authority. At each point where you have approached closely to the limit and know that you are likely to have to exceed it, or that you have exceeded it already, you have to ensure between negotiating sessions that you clear your lines with appropriate people and can continue along your set course, having gained approval for the actions you have taken and are likely to take.

Good negotiators will not be afraid of being charged with authority, often beyond that which they might normally carry. If they are afraid, they do not have the self-confidence and aplomb to be really competent and successful and to progress into ever more complex and demanding negotiations. The skill is to find your own level, giving adequate challenge and exposing you to enough risk to charge you with the drive to succeed but not so much that the personal exposure and possibly the fear of failure cause you to take too cautious a line.

In selecting negotiators for training, the principal requirement in this respect is to ensure that the person concerned has the willingness to take on the next challenge but not too much confidence or self-belief as to place the deal at risk.

Figure 2.1 illustrates the relationships between an individual's search for power and willingness to accept risk and how that can influence their suitability as a negotiator.

CHANGING ETHICS

Some years ago, if you had mentioned post-tender negotiation – discussing the terms proposed in a contractor's or supplier's competitive bid in order to improve on them – to officials in the UK central government sector they would have first thrown up their hands in horror and then have you thrown out. PTN was unethical in principle and could not be countenanced as it left the public sector negotiator highly exposed to being corrupted or to accusations of corruption. There was a considerable fear of the process as well as a considerable suspicion of it.

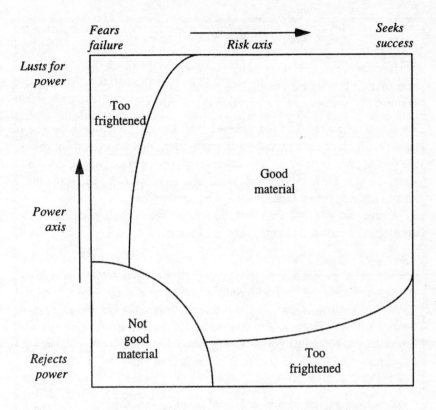

Figure 2.1 The risk/power matrix: identifying negotiator potential.

Nowadays, ask a central government official who is involved in market testing of services or the procurement of goods or services what are the stages they will be following and PTN will be an integral part of their process. It will not seem odd to them or need a second reference or explanation. It has become as normal a way of life as producing the initial specification – nobody would ever consider going out to tender without it.

On another front, economic recessions have a major impact on peoples' attitudes to ethics. And ethical standards do not necessarily return to where they stood prior to a recession. Approaches once learned and used to advantage will remain in one's armoury long after the real need for them has passed.

Gaps in the Specification

During the recession that hit particularly the UK but also much of the rest of the world during the early 1990s a skill which had been around for many years came much more into its own.

At times when tenders for business can be submitted with reasonable profit margins and still be won, bidders will choose their price according to a number of factors, of which one might be the competence with which they feel the specification and contract terms have been written. If they view the terms as somewhat loose or ill considered, they may include something in their quotations to allow for uncertainties and potential additional work.

However, when times are tough and people are cutting bids to the bone simply to keep their staff in work and gain some cash flow, attitudes change. What had been the ethics of a business – a fair job for a fair return – can be thrown out. Then the gaps and weaknesses in a specification become means of making extra. The opportunity to make claims for anything remotely perceived as different or extra work may be pounced upon and developed to deliver as much extra cash as possible.

On the return of more balanced trading conditions, when the power does not lie apparently so much in the hands of buyers, the providers of services may well not return to their old ethic of fair play and reasonableness. They have discovered that there is money to be made from a quite different business ethic. Some will continue in the ways they learned during the recession and that will tilt the competitive balance so that all players in the market will have to review where they stand and compete in a different way.

CONSIDERING YOUR 'OPPONENT'

It is unlikely that any sportsperson would disagree with the statement that it is unwise to underestimate your opponent. That seems to need neither explanation nor justification. But equally as important, but perhaps not quite as obvious, is that you should not *overestimate* the opponent either. Why? What harm can come if you as a negotiator indulge in overestimation?

○ You may spend an excessive and uneconomic amount of time in preparing for the meeting.

○ You could put in an unnecessarily large or overly senior team.

○ Your approach in discussions may be slower and more cautious than you need.

○ You may allow fear to override good reason.

○ You may be looking unduly long for something that is not there.

"Don't over-estimate them son, they may look frightening but they scare easy"

There are, however, some aspects of your attitudes towards your opponent that might be considered as overestimation but which are worth keeping in mind.

At the outset of any negotiation – and certainly well before you are due to meet face to face across the table – it is sensible to assume that your opponent is well trained in the art. That will encourage you to plan carefully, collect the right type and level of information and handle yourself with an appropriate balance of caution and risk throughout. Perhaps it will turn out not to be true that your opponent has both been well trained and has benefited from the training, but that may become clear as you proceed. There is no harm in starting out on the safer route.

BODY LANGUAGE

A skilled negotiator can send you false signals. So personally, I try to pick up on the words and messages rather than visual signs.

David Radcliffe, Managing Director, Hogg Robinson (Travel) Ltd.

Much has been made by many of those who write and teach about interactions between people of the value of body language. Unfortunately, the subject has now become far too well publicised for it to be highly significant to negotiators. There are views that you can read your opponent's position, reactions and opinions from body signals; that by careful trained observation of responses to the points you are making, the enquiries you are putting and even to your own body language, you can obtain highly relevant information about the other side's thoughts.

This has always worried me as a concept. What, for example, if your opponent has also heard of the importance of body language? What if he is actually trying to send misleading signals? What if you are giving away more messages than you should because you are concentrating on reading the secret signs rather than concealing your own?

Bewilderment by Body Language

Some years ago I worked in a company which made engineering products which others bought to put into their finished goods. I was responsible for managing the development of a new factory which would produce a completely new product. Our sales team was to visit a potential customer who was quite close to buying and they felt that our presentation would be more effective if I went along and explained how my new factory and new equipment would produce the high quality they needed, give them flexibility to change their orders at short notice and ensure that there was adequate capacity to satisfy their ever-changing needs. It was to be a plum order that would give the new factory a flying start and fully justify the decision to proceed.

Our team leader was an experienced salesman who had prepared thoroughly and knew his product and his costings inside out. He also knew about body language; perhaps, indeed, he knew a bit too much about it. I was the new boy in the team and therefore somewhat suspect so he gave me a briefing on what to do and what not to do. I was also charged with the task of observing the body language of the customers as I would have a relatively small part to play in the real negotiations.

The other side came along with five people, we went with four. The meeting lasted in all for around three and a half hours and was well structured and well controlled by my senior colleague. I was aware that my role came relatively early and that, once I had made my presentation, I was to respond to questions as they were selected and passed to me by our team leader. That was all over rather early on and I could concentrate on the body signals.

It did not take long for me to realise that there were serious conflicts on the other side. When we were putting a key point, some of them would lean forward in interest while others would show either lack of response or positive disinterest. I could not even identify consistency from, for example, the finance representative on financial issues. Clearly, their whole team was in utter disarray and we were running rings around them. But it did not seem to be going that way in the negotiation itself.

As you will have guessed, their side was exhibiting a whole range of reactions to everything. Different people had different perceptions of the points under discussion. They were not parading them in front of us as they were a good effective team. But anything that could be read from their body language would be as likely to be confusing as it would be useful.

The whole thing was put in perspective when I had disappointed our team leader by reporting back that I had made neither head nor tail of their reactions. I then spoke to another team member who responded 'Oh, Jack told you that, did he? Yes I suppose he would. He has a bee in his bonnet about body language and is always looking for someone to convince.'

Table 2.1 shows some of the more usual assumptions about body language, as well as some of the meanings you might wish to place upon the signals that you will see.

So is there any value to negotiators in reading body language? Yes, there is, but the importance of the subject is frequently overstated. If you were the only person to have heard of the signals and indications that can be obtained from body language, then it would be of immense value to you. Unfortunately, this is unlikely to be the case and you should certainly not rely to any significant degree on body signals.

The value of body language to a negotiator lies in gradually and progressively building a picture, in picking up general signals and overall impressions. It is unwise to take too much account of specific signals or of signals that are too obvious. But you will find that some overall messages can be read and some overall impressions be gained. Certainly, body language can be useful in reinforcing messages that you have received through other indicators. Just do not place too much importance on it.

And make sure that you do not inadvertently give away indicators that you would rather have kept from the other side.

Before we move off the subject of body language, there is one aspect that is worth pursuing – facial expression. The world's best poker players never allow themselves any change in their facial expression at all. If they start with a slight smile, then a slight smile remains there throughout the game. If they start looking glum, then glum it is. For them, it is far safer not to permit flickers of change of

Table 2.1 Possible messages from body language signals

Body language signal	*Possible meaning*
O Leans forward while making a point	— is feeling confident.
	— is really interested.
	— taking you into confidence.
	— about to become aggressive.
O Leans back as you make a point	— is unhappy with this point.
	— is relaxed about this point.
	— wishes to consider carefully.
	— is allowing colleague to take over.
O Smiles at one of your points	— is about to win something.
	— thinks is about to lose something.
	— recognises you are breaking deadlock.
	— is very unhappy about your point.
O Looks surprised at your point	— is surprised.
	— wishes you to believe surprised.
	— was expecting this all along.
	— intends to laugh out this point.
O Reacts aggressively to your point	— felt annoyed by your point.
	— wished to concentrate attention on that point.
	— wished to divert attention from elsewhere.
	— had suddenly remembered a different point.
O And so on	— And so on

expression in case they inadvertently permit one which gives a signal they did not want. And there is no point using such things to persuade your opponent about your hand because that simply would not be achieved, because it would not be believed anyway.

The negotiator should assume that the opponent is in the second division of the world's poker players – that is, not having quite learned to have no expression at all but sometimes attempting to give a specific impression and, less often still, giving away something that was not intended. The problem is, you will not know when it was intentional and when it was not! It remains safer, then, to ignore what your opponent may be signalling by facial expression and pick up the hints from other, more tangible, aspects of the negotiation.

MOODS AND EMOTIONS

Negotiators never have moods. Either good or bad. They may feel like having them, but they don't ever let that get on top of them. They may *indicate* moods but they are always in control and quite deliberately sending the signals that they want to send. If everything in their lives has gone wrong, they never let on to the other side; and if they think that everything is going wrong with the negotiation and that it is all because they have messed it all up, they never let on to the other side.

And, of course, they never have emotions or worries either. They never allow extraneous factors like a relative being seriously ill or their house falling down to affect them to even the slightest extent when negotiating. It is quite amazing how many top sportspeople can block things out which they do not want to think about while engaged in their business. One can only marvel at the snooker player who can calmly pot balls so that he can finish the match in time to get to hospital and see his wife produce their first child. If they could not exert such control over their feelings they could not regularly be at the top, not because so many babies are born but because a myriad of other worries would also overwhelm them.

All this sounds far too good to be true. How do such iron-willed people, such paragons of virtue, ever become negotiators? Of course, few of them do. But we all have to aspire to their standards. We all have to overcome for short times our own feelings and outlooks and focus totally on the negotiation in hand. Whether our moods, emotions and worries are driven by the stage or outcome of a negotiation, or by something completely separate from it – be it at home or at work – they must be seen as quite separate from what has to be done to put together the deal that is being sought.

Is this really possible when we are, after all, only human? It is only partially possible, and the extent depends on the characteristics intrinsic in each of us. The reason for highlighting the factor here is to identify that the *objective* must be to blot out moods and personal factors from influencing our work on a negotiation. The objective must be to allow no personal feelings to affect our work or our approach. It is the extent to which that objective is achieved that indicates how effective we have been at isolating our personal feelings from the technical job in hand.

There will be many readers who will respond that they have seen successful negotiators who have willingly exhibited moods during negotiations and have been perfectly willing to allow the opposition to know when they were happy with the route things were taking and when they were somewhat less happy. This is in no way in conflict with the paragraphs above – as long as those particular negotiators were fully in control of their mood indications. There is no reason at all why you should not drive your mood indicators to your benefit. There are very many good reasons why you should not let your moods drive you.

AGGRESSION

There are hawks in negotiating teams who believe that the best approach is the strongest and that if you hit the other side hard and forcefully follow up, they will be reeling back long enough for you to do just the deal you want. This approach works if you hold many of the cards, have total control over the delivery of the goods or service and have little regard for doing business with the other party again. However, few of us have the opportunity to negotiate from such a position. In any event, forcing your wishes on a weak opponent is hardly negotiating in the way we are looking at it. The line 'give me your money or I'll shoot you' would not be recognised as a serious negotiating opener. It only becomes that if you in turn can point out that behind the gunman is your colleague with an even bigger gun pointed at him. We will not address here the subtle and not so subtle art of threats and deterrents but will restrict ourselves to negotiations between willing parties, each of whom has something to gain and either of whom could walk away from the deal if it was not meeting the predetermined necessary requirements.

Does aggression have a place in negotiating? Yes, indeed it does. It may be simply posturing, it may be based on something real, but it has a position.

Aggression can throw opponents off track or encourage them not to approach particular issues or press them too hard. It can cause them to hurry through because they do not much care to be dealing with you. It can draw the focus of attention from something you did not want looked at in detail and allow time to be spent elsewhere – on topics you are more willing to have examined. It can, of course, also bring aggression out of your opponents, and then what have you achieved but two parties who set out to find the basis of a deal and ended up shouting at each other and seeking more and more ways to score points. If that is what you seek, don't become a negotiator but go into politics!

For what can war but endless war still breed?

Milton, *On the Lord General Fairfax.*

As with every approach, every trick, every stunt that can be pulled in negotiation, there is another side. Aggression might well give away which areas you do not want examined. It might encourage the other side to walk away from a deal you really did want simply because they cannot envisage dealing with you and trusting you. It may cause you to focus inappropriately if you have to pursue a particular style even when the value of it has become limited. When you are dealing with reasonably competent negotiators on the other side, aggression put up as an artificial front will cause almost as many problems to the aggressor as to the intended victim, and possibly more.

Where there is perceived to be a need for genuine aggression, it is better if the person playing the part is brought into the team while such an approach is needed and is then excluded from it to enable progress to be made. The aggressor is then known by all to be in reserve, on the basis that, if the deal is not done, the unpleasantness will return. In this case the aggressor may be the immediate superior of the negotiator or someone who has no direct connection but is part of the negotiating team from time to time.

On the other hand, although many would accept the veracity of the view that:

The meek shall inherit the earth.

Bible, Matthew 5.

it is inconceivable that they will inherit by relying entirely on negotiation.

The Builder Who Would Bite Off Your Head

On construction work, it is usual to hold back some of the money due to the contractor until faults are rectified at the end of the job. This is known as 'retention'. It can often represent the difference between loss and profit.

I was asked to attend a meeting to discuss remedial work on a complex scheme whose owner had been put into receivership. My client wanted the work finished so that the property could be sold, while the contractor – whom we understood to be in financial difficulty – thought he had done enough to secure his money.

We agreed that I would front for our team and that our strategy for the first meeting would be to obtain information to assess prior to the next meeting. My colleague had ensured that the meeting could not last more than 45 minutes.

Three people from the contractor's side attended – I will call them Leader, Numbers Man and Aggressor, for obvious reasons.

We were still taking our places around the table when Aggressor, who was immediately opposite me, rose from his chair, leaned across the table and started to scream abuse at me, thinking I was the receiver responsible for holding back his money. I have been called some unpleasant things in my time but this was an exceptionally skilled performance; it went on for only around 10 minutes but seemed like 10 hours. If some of the things he said just happened to be true, I took that to be a coincidence. It you fire off everything, you are bound to hit something.

At one point, Aggressor paused for breath, Leader took him by the elbow and directed him gently back to his seat. Leader then emphasised that it must be clear how intensely they felt about this issue. He presented their case in a calm and rational way, referring frequently to Numbers Man. Always in reserve was Aggressor, who was itching to get up again and continue. Leader kept him in check from time to time with gentle touches on his arm but released him twice more for short spurts when it was felt that we were not being reasonable.

What did this approach achieve for the contractor? No advantage, because we were not frightened into giving way. A number of disadvantages because:

○ we did not raise certain issues if we expected them to be emotive − they would have preferred to have everything exposed and discussed;
○ we often listened in silence to their points, rather than say that we did not accept all or part of them;
○ in spite of our training, we felt annoyed rather than conciliatory;
○ the meeting progressed nothing and did not increase our likelihood of settling at a level that the contractor wanted.

LIKED OR RESPECTED

I like people and I like them to like me, but I wear my heart where God put it, on the inside.

F. Scott Fitzgerald, *The Last Tycoon.*

Trying to do business and agree a deal with someone you clearly do not like is difficult. Personal conflicts become bars to logic and the will to win becomes distorted beyond sound business sense. There is, however, a gulf of difference between not specifically liking someone and actually disliking them.

Some negotiators set out to be difficult and even unpleasant, holding the view that they will drive their opponent into a corner and grab the maximum benefit from the negotiation. They have no regard for any continuity of business and often even less regard for whether the opponent can or will deliver under the deal they have agreed. They deserve all they get and, in the long run, they will get very little except opponents who approach them with the same aggression and unpleasantness. That is rarely in the interest of either party in serious negotiation.

You are in business as a negotiator to win the respect of the opposition, but not necessarily until the negotiation is over. Whatever the other side thinks of you during the discussions, as long as there is not positive dislike, matters very little. What the same people think of you after the discussion, when the deal is signed up and to be delivered, is another matter. If you have not by then won at least a degree of respect, you have probably not won the deal that you should have won.

You are not there to be liked, nor to be disliked. You are there to be respected in retrospect if not before. Just imagine how well the top sports people would perform if they always wanted their opponents to like them. Steffi Graf would not play the lob if her opponent could not get to it; Nick Faldo would hit his ball into the rough if his opponent had, just to stay with him; Magic Johnson would give the ball to the other team every time he had scored a basket.

Many of the personal characteristics that might go to make up a good negotiator are summarised in Figure 2.2 which shows that a mix of personality traits is needed but the precise blend can be drawn from a wide spectrum. Selection of a negotiator for any particular circumstances should reflect both the outcome that is sought and the opposition that is likely to be met.

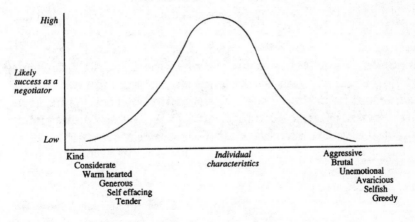

Figure 2.2 The negotiator's blend of characteristics.

TELLING THE TRUTH

O what a tangled web we weave,
When first we practise to deceive!

Sir Walter Scott, *Marmion*.

Sir Walter was putting over an excellent piece of advice to any negotiator. Once you have set out to deceive, you have to maintain a web of deceit that will sustain you. Quite apart from any ethical considerations about lying in business, there is much to be said for not creating your own web that you will then have to maintain. For one thing, maintaining the web will result in you having to transfer your focus from the activity on which you should be concentrating to one on which you should not.

If we accept that telling lies deliberately can lead at least to inconvenience and worse still to defocusing you from your main objective, does that mean that you always have to tell 'the truth, the whole truth and nothing but the truth'? No, of course it does not. There is no point laying out your whole case truthfully at the start of a negotiation; it will begin to emerge at the times you judge aspects of it to be most appropriate. And you may be aware at times that your opponent could be slightly misled about your position, not because you have been untruthful but perhaps because you have not revealed all and perhaps because the other team has jumped to an unjustified conclusion on the facts available.

We come back here to the issue of ethics. You and you alone can decide when you have crossed the ethical divide between allowing your opponent to be misled and leading him back to an impression based on a more honest representation of the facts. The balance may be within your power to influence and, if it is, you will have to address in your mind the balance between integrity and gain. Nobody can influence you towards any specific balance because the circumstances will vary, but Mark Twain seems to have got it right:

> *There was many things which he stretched,*
> *but mainly he told the truth.*

> Mark Twain, *The Adventures of Huckleberry Finn*.

KNOW YOUR LIMITATIONS

Nobody would deny that when they become tired or hungry they do not perform at their best. Many would also agree that there comes a time for of us in any complicated matter when we would like to say: 'I need to step back from this and just see where I have got to.'

We know that if we go on, things will become more confused and we will not perform at the peak of comprehension and response. Just as this happens in many aspects of life, we have to recognise that it happens in negotiations. The macho negotiator who insists on working through the night to revise a presentation and the entire approach that will be followed the next day is not doing any favours to anyone except the opposition.

Into the Nigerian Night

A team of negotiators representing a UK consortium had gone out to Lagos in Nigeria to negotiate for a contract to finance, design, construct and operate a new transport system for the capital. They were in competition with two other consortia and had a rough time from the client – a ministry of the Nigerian government – who had pursued a quite different range of topics than those on which they were suitably prepared.

It appeared that all of the negotiating teams had similarly rough rides because the UK team was invited back the following day to re-present their case to the ministry negotiators. Other information they came upon indicated that the opposition had been one German and one French team. The Germans had not been invited back but the French had. It was clearly now a close two-horse race. The French were to re-submit at 9.00 o'clock and the British at 11.30.

The UK team went off to its hotel to work through the points raised by the client. When they started to identify other points which they thought might be raised, they recognised that they had a long night's work ahead of them. There were six on the team and the self-appointed (but importantly, universally accepted) team leader immediately dispatched three of the team to bed. They were mortified that it was felt that their services could be dispensed with. What had they done to deserve being cut out at this late stage? Had they not been instrumental in reaching the position of being one of only two bidders? Yes, they had been willing to accept this individual as unofficial team leader but what right did he have to send them packing so unceremoniously at such a critical moment?

But that, of course, was not the purpose of sending them away. They were to get a good night's sleep. The others would work through and prepare the new presentation by morning. All would meet for an early breakfast to go through the night-workers' thoughts and finalise the presentation. If possible, the night-workers

> would then grab whatever sleep they could before attending the presentation.
>
> The night-sleepers would drive the presentation and deal with most of the questions, The tired group would only come in if they were really needed. It would have been preferable if their presence could have been avoided altogether, but that was judged inappropriate as they had specific technical knowledge that might be needed.
>
> The French team paraded first. All were exhausted, having worked through the night and they were not successful in winning the contract.
>
> How much was the UK success down to their tactics? We will never know. But their approach certainly enhanced their ability to deal with a difficult negotiation on which a very substantial order depended.

Whether you are alone or a team member, the message is the same. Make sure that you are in the right physical shape to handle the negotiation that faces you. If it is expected to be particularly gruelling, then you have to be in exceptionally good shape before it starts and you have to ensure that there are breaks at suitable intervals for you to recharge your personal batteries. It is not a sign of weakness to need to do so. It is a sign of self-management, control, awareness and calm. Never try to outdo the opposition in the macho stakes. There is simply no point. You can manage the negotiation perfectly well without taking the risk that you will come out better than them. Always bear in mind that your opponent may, in any event, have predicted a physical element to the combat and have got himself far fitter than you. Do not take the analogy between negotiation and sport to such extremes!

HOME AND AWAY

We will investigate more fully in later chapters many of the issues arising out of the debate about playing home or away but this is an appropriate point at which to consider your personal position in this respect.

Some people feel much happier when they are in familiar surroundings; they feel that they are in control, that they have not been hassled in getting to the other person's location, that they did not have additional stresses of unfamiliarity placed on their shoulders. Such people – and we probably all feel this way at some time and in some situations – should ensure that they play at home; that the opposition visit them and that they are met on comfortable and familiar ground.

There will be times during negotiations when you will need to visit the other side's premises, perhaps you have agreed to take it in turns to host the discussions, perhaps you need to see their facilities, perhaps you can travel much more readily than they, but you can keep such instances to a minimum if you are unhappy or not relaxed with them. You can also seek to ensure that only the less important factors are considered at such sessions, leaving you to handle the more important facets where you feel happier.

The important thing here is to understand both your own feelings and how you should respond to them. It is less important to understand why you feel the way you do – you might get to grips with that issue more at your leisure – whereas the crucial thing is to identify how it impacts upon any particular negotiation. Appreciate what you want to do early on in the process and arrange things so that you achieve your own ends. It may turn out in the final analysis to be quite unimportant, but you should nevertheless invoke your own wishes at the outset.

LAYOUT OF THE ROOM

You will all have come across the personnel and human relations teachings that recommend that you do not conduct, for example, appraisal interviews across a desk. Instead, they propose that you sit around a low table so that you are self-perceived as equals, or that you sit in armchairs that encourage you to be relaxed.

The same theories are often drawn into negotiation debates. There is no harm in this if the justifications for selecting specific arrangements are related to the negotiation in question and do not become rules to live by. Whatever layout you choose, do it for a reason that you understand and that makes sense to the circumstances in which you are operating. If you want to sit at opposite sides of a conference table, do so. The arrangement will be very familiar to both parties and not cause any particular hangups. Indeed, I have always felt that it is rather artificial to meet a potential new supplier whilst all lounging around in comfy leather armchairs!

Layout and environment should be functions of:

○ the norms adopted by the organisation;

○ the way in which you usually work and feel comfortable;

○ the image you wish to put over;

○ how comfortable and relaxed you want them to be;

○ the facilities that are readily available;

○ and, of course, the amount of paper you have to consult.

I do not know of a negotiation where the layout has been of major significance to the outcome. It can have but a minor influence. The principal concern is that you do not spend too much time working on something that may not have any impact at all on the outcome.

'I'VE BEEN NEGOTIATING FOR 35 YEARS...'

Whenever I hear this said to trainees or on seminars, I recoil in horror. It is usually followed by the statement that '... so there's nothing I'm going to learn now, is there?' If it is my opponent who tells me that he has been in the business for an enormous number of years, I am delighted. I know that there are patterns into which the debate is likely to fall. Naturally, I will remain cautious in case it is a trick to entice me into a set line of thought, but it rarely is.

> *You have not had thirty years' experience... You have had one year's experience 30 times.*
>
> J. L. Carr, *The Harpole Report*.

What is the point of this message? It is that experience alone is simply not enough. Indeed, experience alone is dangerous and possibly disastrous. But experience flavoured with learning and awareness and which retains the willingness to learn even from someone who is perhaps only just starting in the business is very powerful. Do not rely on your experience alone, nor solely on the experience of others. But how can you improve while you are building up those many years of experience? You can do this through:

○ formal and informal training, including reading;

○ obtaining coaching from others whose views you respect;

○ yourself coaching others less experienced than you;

○ undertaking live negotiations – on-the-job self-training;

○ reviewing a completed negotiation and analysing the best and worst points.

INSTINCT AND INTUITION

Perhaps all of this self-understanding and self-appraisal results in you taking too formal, regimented and standardised an approach to your negotiations. It should not. Successful negotiators do indeed have all of these factors under control but will also be willing to take risks and back their own intuitions. There will be many times when you feel that you would like to try a particular strategy or approach but cannot be definitive about why. You just have the feeling that it could work; perhaps other attempts to gain agreement have not worked and you want to go for something different. Try it; take the chance. As long as you are aware of the magnitude of the risk and the potential downside if you are wrong, you may still decide to go with it.

In the first chapter, emphasis was placed on the sporting nature of the negotiation process. The best sportspeople have occasions when they have to back their judgement, often at short notice, and draw on their training and experience in taking spur-of-the-moment decisions. If they are right, they come away with gold medals; if they are wrong they may well sink into oblivion. But they are willing to take the chance and must always believe that they can achieve gold. So it is with negotiators. Never lose the willingness – or perhaps even the desire – to try something new, to go out on a limb, to take a few risks and to achieve more than would ever have been possible otherwise. If you do lose this flair for excitement and challenge, then give up negotiation and settle for a quiet desk job. But don't blame me.

FLEXIBILITY

It is appropriate at this point to reiterate the theme of flexibility. We have seen already that:

> *The golden rule is that there are no golden rules.*
>
> George Bernard Shaw, *Maxim for Revolutionists.*

Whatever course you have chosen to plot through a negotiation, be willing to scrap it if the facts and circumstances demonstrate clearly that it is not working or will not work as you had intended. Make either great or small changes as needed, but do not necessarily throw out everything of your approach because one bit is wrong. You require the confidence to scrap but also the confidence to retain.

In this respect, negotiation is no different from general management. The same advice could be given to the manager faced with a problem where things were not going to plan. Flexibility is not a skill unique to negotiators, but is certainly one that is required of all negotiators if they are to be successful.

Let us review for a moment how this might fit with our sporting analogy. No individual or team has ever won anything worth having without the ability to face up to their opponents, judge how they are playing the game, play to the opponents' perceived weaknesses and work to counter their strengths. No player who has failed to dominate the game and take full advantage of his own strengths has ever come out on top. When you see the other team's selection, you consider whether it might be most appropriate to change yours; when the other team's left-wing player seems to be dropping in excellent centres consistently from the left, you strengthen your defence on that side.

In negotiating, you need all these aspects of flexibility and more. You also need to bear in mind a point that was made earlier and which does run through this book as a theme – namely that you have to decide at the outset just how far you wish to push your opponent. Whatever deal you think you have done, the party with whom you have been negotiating must be able to deliver and must want to continue to deliver. The opposing sportsperson may feel well beaten but must have enjoyed the game and have got enough out of it to want a return match.

"Frankly, I'm going to expect a lot more flexibility in future"

SELF-EVALUATION

There are many proprietary self-evaluation tests on the market, and training courses in such subjects as selling skills, face-to-face negotiating and industrial relations often include modules where such tests are run. To be of most value, they should be conducted by trained and experienced people but even then they can be but a pointer to the forces which drive people and the ways in which they would react in different circumstances.

To negotiators, such indicators have value if they assist in the process of understanding one's own personal requirements and in being able to develop at least some evaluation of the person or people who will be facing you. Many of the tests identify around six

Table 2.2 The six-pack of personal drivers

The Driver	*How the Driver Influences Behaviour*
Authority	The extent to which we seek influence, authority and power in our working environment and relationships. This may be manifested in taking responsibility for others, or for the actions of a group, or for directing the resources of a large entity.
Success	How much we are driven by the need for success and to be able to feel that we have achieved something truly worthwhile, perhaps even something that nobody else in the organisation could have achieved.
Appreciation	Our need for our successes and achievements to be recognised by our peers, our subordinates and our superiors. Appreciation does not have to bring immediate rewards; the knowledge that appreciation has been shown will often suffice for a considerable period.
Membership	Our need to be part of a group or team and be recognised as a contributor member. This includes the need to 'belong' and to become involved in the activities of the team as well as simply being a member. One's position within the team is governed by the other personal factors and drivers.
System	Covering our need to operate within a defined set of rules and parameters as well as the extent to which we wish to impose order and discipline on our surroundings. This may manifest itself in a desire to keep well-ordered files and have everything clearly documented and tagged, but is reflected in logical thought processes that ensure that important issues are clearly separated and dealt with systematically.
Security	The desire to feel safety in what we do and avoid personal risk. This might be seen in the wish to have rules to work to, so that there is no personal risk in making a decision, in agreeing a contract with a regular 'safe' supplier, or of ensuring that each step in a negotiation has the approval of someone more senior.

key features that relate to our individual needs. I like to think of them as a personal six-pack of factors that make up our personalities and affect our behaviour. It is important to note that the way in which we are assessed at home can be quite different from how our work colleagues might judge us.

The personal drivers were set out in Table 2.2.

It is not appropriate in this book to pursue this in great detail but it will suffice to highlight these factors and invite negotiators to consider where they believe they might fit on, say, a scale of 1 to 5 on each of them. By all means ask people for whom you have respect and to whom you will listen to discuss the factors with you, but do ensure that they will not simply tell you what they think you want to hear!

If you wish to delve deeper into the topic, then obtain one of the test sets which a number of specialist consultants operate and have them work through them properly.

Before leaving this topic, it is worth just looking for a moment at the significance of it to the people you are negotiating with.

In many cases, an individual opponent may be known to both the negotiator and to others in the organisation. If that is the case, it may be possible to build up a picture of that person's drivers on the basis of this prior knowledge. Clearly, this has to be done with caution because you may not have seen very much that is real in that person before, or may have seen simply one side of their character. But these caveats do not mean that you cannot obtain value from such an analysis.

Take each heading in turn and pool all available information about the person and attempt to identify the extent to which you can draw a conclusion. For example, does he seek safety in being able to prove that you have done exactly this type of work before; does he like to feel important and to demonstrate that nobody else takes the decisions; does a thorough and systematic approach and presentation of pedantic detail impress him; should you take a somewhat matey and friendly line or would it be more appropriate to be cold, businesslike and exhibiting no human feelings?

Do not go overboard on this – as with many of the techniques and approaches described in this book, things should be handled gently and the whole set of pointers and indicators should be used to help in your strategy and tactics. The evaluation of personal drivers is but one of many things that will help you piece together the jigsaw.

A THOUGHT ON COACHING

Jennifer Capriati's father has apparently admitted to making mistakes in bringing up his troubled daughter. 'I messed up with Jennifer because I put too much pressure on her,' Stefano Capriati was quoted as saying . . . 'but I didn't know how good she really was and I wanted to find out by putting her up against stronger players.'

The Independent, 10 June 1994.

It will be clear that there is a lot to learn before one can become a truly competent negotiator. Less experienced and skilled negotiators can be developed on the job by perceptive encouragement, coaching and exposure to new situations. The manager must take risks by giving increasing authority and then not overriding it when something seems to have gone wrong – you have to live with that. As with so many things, small steps are best, with each providing the opportunity for at least one new learning experience. Excessive steps, and those which require too much learning in one go, can destroy confidence, create doubt in the mind of the trainee and even bring into doubt in the minds of others that the right person was undertaking that particular discussion.

Small but positive steps will enable the individual to develop and the organisation to accept the risk and exposure that the manager has decided are appropriate.

PATIENCE

It will be clear that there is much to consider, much to learn and much to do before facing the other side across the table. And the next few chapters will add to the burden of what has to be understood and done before you start the negotiation proper. Is this all really necessary? Indeed it is, but not all at once and not all on every negotiation.

Much of what has been written in this chapter is to emphasise that there are certain characteristics of the successful negotiator that are in all of us. It is a matter of appreciating which they are and using them to the full. Only by knowing yourself, your colleagues and your opponents can you be successful at an art that depends to such a great extent upon interpersonal relationships and on understanding what is motivating and driving the opposing team.

Overall, however, the key requirement is patience. A good negotiation cannot be harried along or hurried. You must take your time,
analyse the position, examine the information, develop the strategy
and play the options until you have your objective in sight. If you
are negotiating for a once-off deal, the experience can be enjoyable.
If you are setting up a long-term partnership or contract, the extra
satisfaction involved in getting just the right deal that will last but
pay dividends for your organisation can be substantial. But it can be
achieved only with patience.

IN SUMMARY

It is worth just pausing for a moment to revisit the key messages
from this chapter. They form a clear basis for the work we will be
examining in subsequent chapters and, although there will be refer-
ences to these points in relation to other matters in the negotiating
process, we will not re-examine them in detail.

- Have a realistic idea of your own strengths, weaknesses and
  characteristics as a negotiator.
- To the best extent you can, ascertain the strengths and weaknesses of your opponent as a person.
- Ensure that you have appropriate authority and know when you
  have overstepped it.
- Read messages from body language and by all means use it; but
  do not let it become over-important in your work as a negotiator.
- Never allow yourself to have moods or emotions; never lose
  your temper; certainly set out to give particular impressions but,
  as with body language, do not become diverted from the prime
  objective.
- Remember that you do not have to be liked; you certainly
  should not be disliked; you should, by the end, be respected.
- Tell some of the truth all of the time.
- Choose the surroundings and layout that suit you and in which
  you feel relaxed.
- Be flexible in your thinking, always.
- Be patient.

If you can keep all of those requirements in mind *and* carry out all of the tasks involved in preparing for the negotiation and executing it successfully, with attention to detail, patience and thoroughness, you will have ascended all the peaks of the art of negotiation.

> *Though the mills of God grind slowly,*
> *yet they grind exceeding small;*
> *Though with patience he stands waiting,*
> *with exactness grinds he all.*

Henry Longfellow, 'Retribution', from the *Sinngedichte* of Friedrich von Logau.

3

Why negotiate?

Negotiation – The action of getting over or round some obstacle by skilful manoevring.

Oxford Dictionary, c1885.

Inherent in this definition is that there is an objective in view when getting over or round the obstacle. We will consider in this chapter the form in which that objective might arise and see how the 'manoevring' might be influenced by that objective. We will first look at some of the reasons why a negotiation might be undertaken.

WHY NEGOTIATE?

Whatever the commercial deal that is being negotiated, there is always one simple objective that should be in the minds of both parties. That is that the purpose of commercial negotiation between different business entities is:

To create an economic benefit for the negotiator's business.

It truly is that simple. You start from whichever point you were at before the negotiation began and your sole objective is to improve your economic position. This term 'economic position' can embrace very many elements that might be negotiated. Most negotiations include an element of price and many writers and lecturers seem to concentrate on that part too heavily. This obscures the fact that there is often more to be gained in a negotiation by ignoring price at the outset and identifying all of the other factors where your economic benefit may be improved. Once you have those clearly in mind, then have look at the price position. It is too easy to become price-oriented and not notice or seek some of the other benefits.

It is important to note that this definition of purpose completely excludes the position in which the people against whom you are negotiating find themselves. You must assume that they have precisely the same overall objective – to improve their economic position at your expense – but that their view of 'improvement' may be along quite different lines and that they may have a quite different way of getting there. We will examine the situation regarding your position and that of these opponents a little later when we look at concepts like win-win and win-lose.

COLLEAGUES

Although a substantial amount of negotiation takes place between people from different organisations, there is perhaps more that is done in one way or another between people from the same organisation, and even from within the same department. When people examine their daily round, they usually identify very large numbers of incidents where they used one form or another of negotiating skill. In such cases the objective is not particularly to gain overall commercial advantage for your organisation but to better the lot of your specific unit within it – perhaps because you feel that to do so is in the best interest of the organisation overall.

Negotiation between colleagues can take place in a wide variety of different circumstances. Any of us could think of numerous examples and identify the responses which were received and which often represented the opening position in the other person's case. Table 3.1 illustrates a few of these.

The important issue here is not how to handle specifically internal negotiations but whether such matters are distinctly different from negotiating with external people. We are all aware that the most capable external negotiators are not necessarily the best at securing for themselves the best advantages and terms within the organisation. This may be because they focus their efforts more on the sport of negotiating rather than simply trying to feather their own nests, or it might be because they can divorce themselves and their personal interests entirely from the external environment of negotiation.

The principles which are dealt with in this book are quite suited to both internal and external negotiation. Remembering that the objective here is not to set out golden rules but to establish guide-lines and a flow of awareness and self-enlightenment, it is reasonable to take all these messages and use them in either type of negotiation.

Table 3.1 Negotiating with colleagues

My position	*Possible opponent's position*
I need more staff to do the work.	We must all seek to be more efficient. Have you a cost/benefit argument? Do you think we can afford such luxuries? Your predecessor didn't. You have no space for them anyway. You must be joking.
I'd like the first two weeks in August.	Who doesn't? Will you cover Christmas, then? We are rather busy at that time. You don't have children at school. Too late, they have been taken. You must be joking.
I need the reports printed for Tuesday evening.	Which Tuesday? Why didn't you warn us about them? Can you do them yourself? I've got four staff sick and one pregnant. I'll never get the materials. You must be joking.
I feel that my work warrants a pay rise.	There are none this year Whose doesn't? I'll try, but I don't hold out much hope. Or else what? Are you really happy working here? You must be joking.

One of the most amusing features that arises in connection with internal negotiation is the annual budget round. Departments bid for budgets for the next year by enhancing their claims to figures considerably above those that they expect to be awarded. The managers of the overall budget round know that this will happen and have generally allocated the sums that they feel are realistic for the following year, based either on their subjective assessment of what might be required and a knowledge of what will be available or on business projections submitted previously.

The amusement in this system is derived from observing the people who spend many hours putting together their enhanced claims and supporting arguments when they have little chance of obtaining even a small part of their exaggerated sums. But in some organisations it happens year after year and will continue to be a time waster for years to come.

If only such organisations would adopt the simplest rules of negotiation, whereby the two parties discuss the ground rules before they start developing complex and detailed arguments, both sides could save many wasted hours, the expectations of staff would not be raised and dashed unnecessarily and much internal friction could be avoided. The requirement is for those involved to learn the principles of negotiation and apply them.

Even in the most extreme of environments of budget setting, however, negotiation expertise can strengthen the hand of the budget-holding manager. A well prepared case with the main arguments rallied and clear-cut objectives is likely to gain more ground than the blatant 'last year plus inflation plus a bit for expansion' approach.

BUYING AND SELLING

A very substantial amount of negotiation training is done from the viewpoints of purchasing officers and sales people. Often there is little differentiation between the skills they need and, at the level of core skills, this may be appropriate. The two sides do, however, need different approaches at the higher levels, particularly as one side needs to be very widely aware of the selling skills element of the negotiation process.

In various industries it is accepted that salespeople have traditionally been better trained in negotiation than have buyers. Too often it has been considered that the buyers had the whip hand in any negotiation because there were plenty of suppliers vying for the business. The lack of wisdom of this attitude has slowly percolated through and nowadays buyers are trained more thoroughly in the arts of negotiation. This has the result of balancing up the skills and enables buyers to realise how weak their previous positions may have been when aspects of a contract were being negotiated.

Since this book addresses many of the basics of negotiation, as well as concepts such as training, coaching and management of negotiators, there are messages for both buyers and sellers in it. However, some elements will clearly have greater application to buyers rather than sellers, and vice versa. Each reader should derive benefit appropriate to their present and perceived future positions.

In the case of both buyers and sellers, it is important to recognise that the negotiation starts at or even before the first meeting, even if this is ostensibly to discuss only broad parameters. Every exchange between parties should be recognised as a stage in negotiation. At every step, the parties will be trying to give signals and information to the other side and will attempt to elicit information from the other side. Early on, buyers will be obtaining as much background as possible to inform their subsequent choices, while the sellers will be seeking to find out the ultimate user's needs and to influence both the specification and the route to be followed in procurement. This can be a time when either party can too casually give away negotiating strength that they would have made considerable efforts to have kept at a later stage.

Figure 3.1 shows the types of information that a salesperson might be attempting to elicit from a buyer or other contact within a potential target. At each stage, from the initial introduction onwards, there are opportunities to obtain both soft and hard information that might be useful as contacts progress. There are two factors that are not identified in the chart but which equally form part of this process. These are that:

O prior to the introductory visit, the salesperson should have obtained as much relevant information as was available, in order to make the first personal contact more productive;

O the purpose should be to collect relevant information – which may be interpreted quite loosely if there are a number of possible deals on offer – and particularly that which relates to the deal immediately sought.

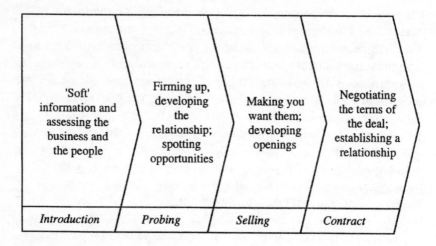

Introduction	Probing	Selling	Contract
'Soft' information and assessing the business and the people	Firming up, developing the relationship; spotting opportunities	Making you want them; developing openings	Negotiating the terms of the deal; establishing a relationship

Figure 3.1 Stages in negotiation – the salesperson.

As long as the very first contact and the initiation of a debate between two parties is recognised as the first stage of a negotiation, and is treated appropriately, then there is no reason why it cannot be highly constructive from the viewpoint of both parties. After all, neither side wishes to spend time considering the opportunities being offered if they are fruitless from their point of view. It is better for both to identify this as early as possible and agree to break off in a friendly way and try to do business on another issue later.

USER'S AND PROVIDER'S NEEDS

It is worth examining for a moment the position that arises when negotiators are not negotiating directly for deals that arise within or impact upon the areas they manage, but as agents for other people. Such circumstances arise frequently when salespeople and buyers are negotiating with each other – the buyer is empowered to negotiate by virtue of holding a central position in a purchasing department and having specific procurement skills and buyer/seller negotiating training; the salesperson visits other firms to negotiate to sell them products or services that will be provided by others in the seller's organisation.

In such situations, it is not uncommon for negotiations to be pursued by buyers and sellers together with scant regard for what it was that the original user had sought or even what the vendor's organisation can provide. Negotiation can take on a life of its own, with positions being adopted, rituals pursued and scraps fought over. Often, these factors on the buyer's side are of no relevance to the ultimate user of the goods or services and the issues being debated and may even result in a deal that is detrimental to his interests. Similarly, the vendor may have lost sight of what he was trying to achieve on the part of his own organisation and simply pursues the order for the sake of obtaining yet more business, at whatever price.

How, then, can you ensure that, on your side of the negotiation at least, this often quite difficult state of affairs is avoided? Only by:

O ensuring that the individual or each member of the team fully appreciates the objectives of the users or providers of the goods or services; and

O that the need of the organisation is recognised and kept in mind during each stage of the negotiation.

If we consider the negotiator in general to be the agent of a principal who is either the direct provider or user of the goods or services, then it is that negotiator's concern to ensure a full understanding of the needs of that principal and to ascertain that they have been taken fully into account in all aspects that are discussed. In effect, the negotiator is not empowered to agree to anything that does not satisfy the requirements specified by that principal or which falls outside a range of parameters that have been defined.

Is the negotiator simply the technician in the process, merely the recipient of instructions to be carried out? Not at all. The true position is quite the opposite. The competent negotiator who is called upon to act on behalf of a principal will:

O use the full range of subtleties, experience and training to achieve the ends of the principal and the organisation as a whole;

O identify by enquiry and probing what are the real needs of the principal, which parameters are absolutely firm and which might be flexible, which elements of the deal which is being sought are inviolate and which have differing degrees of flexibility;

○ at an early stage form an idea of the key issues which are likely to arise and where the opponents might wish to seek movement; these will normally be discussed with the principal in case any important elements have been overlooked;

○ fully understand those aspects where apparently small changes to the principal's wishes may yield significant dividends in negotiating terms.

So the skilled negotiator is the key person here, recognised by the principal as able to do the best deal and take full advantage of what flexibility there is. But that will not come about unless the negotiator recognises that the role is one of service rather than leadership.

Before leaving this area, there is one further point that is worth addressing with regard to negotiating on behalf of a principal. We have seen how the skilled negotiator identifies the correct position from which to conduct the discussion, having ensured a full appreciation of the principal's aims and objectives and understanding the point at which it may be necessary to involve the principal in the debate, but what if the other party has not been so efficient and has no effective appreciation of the business objectives behind their side of the negotiation? This is yet another skill that competent negotiators are expected to develop.

One objective of early discussions, when general enquiries are being made and positions are being defined, is to ascertain just how much your opponent knows about his side of the business and how far things can be allowed to develop before they should be encouraged to seek clarification or even direction from their principal. There is little point spending many hours in discussing, arguing and finalising a deal that is rejected when the opponent has returned to base and discovered that it is not the deal that his principals will accept. It is incumbent upon the negotiator to ascertain not only that a full and comprehensive understanding has been obtained of his own side's requirements, but that the other side has at least an adequate knowledge and appreciation of what is being discussed.

The Pet Plan Deal

Pet Plan is an insurance company that provides cover for show animals. The cover is backed by Lloyds of London, who were concerned that they were not finding the business worthwhile. They were aiming to increase premiums to enable them to continue providing the support to Pet Plan that had been in place. Pet Plan were in turn concerned that many of their breeders would not be willing to pay across the board increases. They were also concerned that an equitable arrangement be reached, giving the Lloyds syndicate an adequate profit and their breeders suitable cover at a fair price. There was a serious potential downside for each of the negotiators. A bad deal from Lloyds would result in them continuously losing money on future business; a bad deal for Pet Plan could result in their breeders moving to another insurer.

Both sides collected significant amounts of supporting data – and then argued over the relevance of each other's – and set about finding a position that they could each support.

The real breakthrough came when Patsy Bloom, the managing director of Pet Plan – who was clearly negotiating on her own behalf and on behalf of her organisation, rather than as an agent for someone else – identified that the core issue was to separate into two lines of business the cover that was provided for cats and that provided for dogs. Claims records were quite different and there had been cross subsidies.

The key issue was to understand that there were in truth two quite different lines of business being negotiated. Separating them would achieve three key objectives, namely that:

○ costs and profitabilities for the two product lines could be isolated and monitored separately;

○ the insurance premiums paid by each type of breeder would more realistically – and therefore fairly – represent the costs of providing the cover;

○ Pet Plan could provide competitive rates in their marketplace for each separate type of business.

Had the negotiator in this case not understood the business she was in, its underlying commercial drivers, and the needs of her clients, this solution would not have been found.

Returning for a moment to the matter of developing an understanding of our own position, the issue is to identify the wider objectives within which those specific to this particular deal must fit. These may relate to many issues of the business, including, for example whether:

○ aspects that might be gained or yielded during this negotiation could have greater impact when viewed more widely – perhaps precedents are being set that are not advantageous to the business as a whole;

○ deals have already been done with this organisation which have an impact upon this one and which should have equal or greater impact than purely local issues;

○ information might be gained during this negotiation that could be of significant value elsewhere – in this event, the negotiation might well be taken down routes which would not otherwise have been chosen.

Other considerations will apply in different circumstances but it is not necessary to pursue them here. Suffice it to say that it is the role of the negotiator, and certainly of the person managing that negotiator, to ensure that any such wider considerations are recognised and taken into account.

It is unwise to assume that any negotiation has no wider ramifications than those that apply directly to the deal in question. It is the negotiator's role to ensure that the full breadth of impact is assessed, understood and allowed for.

When the negotiator *is* the principal, the position is not significantly different. Similar rules and guidance apply since the negotiator has to be fully aware of the impact that the outcome will have on the organisation as a whole, on future business relationships and on their ability to do good and continuing business with their own customers or clients.

WHAT TO NEGOTIATE?

We started this chapter by identifying that the overall objective of commercial negotiation is 'to create an economic benefit for the negotiator's business'. That, of course, is not adequate as an objective for any specific negotiation. Indeed, each negotiation will have a number of separate objectives. These may range, as above, from developing a basis for agreement to doing a deal representing a long-term continuing relationship between two businesses. There are clearly many sub-objectives that might be defined in any one case. These may relate to price – by far the most frequent topic that arises in negotiations – content, quality, availability, service level, guarantees and warranties, and details of the specification of the goods or services under negotiation.

An essential early stage is to ascertain which of these aspects will be negotiated and what targets are to be sought in each case. There will also be a need to ensure that the flexibility within which those targets can be debated must be understood and those which are absolute and cannot be varied. The hawks who tell us all how to negotiate will state that you must assume that:

Everything is negotiable.

But that can easily entail taking your eye off the real issues in order to have everything considered. The 'everything' lobby has plenty of theoretical basis but not much in practice. There will clearly be topics which are not negotiable, either because you are unwilling to move from a certain point and are therefore unwilling to negotiate it, or because there is clear agreement to it already. Opening up such non-negotiables may seem clever and aggressive in theory but will neither fool an experienced opponent nor give rise to additional concessions. The 'everything' lobby thus confuses artificiality and slickness with the real art of negotiation.

If you are clear that there really is little point to negotiating on a specific theme, then do not pretend that there is. The people across the table will mostly see through the sham and not be impressed. You will also divert your valuable preparation and thinking time from those issues where there is value to be gained to those on which there is not.

Should we give any credibility to the 'everything' set? Yes, we should, but only a little. The one thing they do highlight is that everything should at least be considered by you during your preparation stage. You should examine rigorously even those topics which do not at first sight seem susceptible to movement and decide whether your first impression was correct. If not, bring it into the pool of topics to be pursued. But this is the only concession to be granted to such a view.

Against each of your topics that you do feel to be negotiable, objectives must be defined and agreed with those directly concerned. These objectives have to relate to the needs of the ultimate users of the goods or services – which will often not be the negotiators themselves – as well as to the organisation as a whole. Defining objectives is not easy, but there are techniques to help you. One such technique is described below and is then reflected in much of the content of the chapters which follow.

JUST ONCE OR FOR LIFE?

Before taking even the first steps in any particular negotiation it is important to identify whether the course upon which you are embarking is envisaged as setting up:

O a basis of understanding from which you will be able to assess whether a form of relationship might be appropriate to your two organisations;

O a framework within which your organisation and theirs will be able to operate, having established some areas of mutual trust, cooperation and understanding;

O a single deal between you that is not specifically intended to lead to further business activity or a developing relationship but which may do so;

O a long-term relationship or partnership between your organisation and the other party.

If you are the negotiator, you must ensure that you are completely clear as to which aim you are pursuing. If you are unsure, then you should not set out on the negotiation before you have at least enough information and background to begin work on the first of these options – to establish a basis of understanding.

If you are the manager of the negotiator, or the person supervising the preparation that you will draw upon in your own approach to the opposite party, it is again important to ensure that the people working for you appreciate what they are doing and why. This will ensure that their efforts are appropriately oriented and their time effectively used. As we have seen earlier, many aspects of negotiation and managing negotiators are reflected in teachings about general management skills and this is a good example of where this applies.

Basis Of Understanding

'Thank you all for coming to this meeting. I do not expect it to take more than about 45 minutes. Some of you will know already that we have been approached by Swineson and Stye who wish to take over the whole of our procurement and supplies management process. They are offering a structure of prices that they say will be advantageous to us, improved arrangements for stockholding and security of delivery, and a form of quality supervision that they believe will give more reliable and consistent standards throughout.

'We have an outline of the type of service which they are prepared to offer and some of their thoughts as to the benefits that might accrue to us. I will set those out in a few minutes.

'Of course, they have not provided this service to anyone else in quite this form, so we would be something of a trial site for them. You must assess for yourselves whether that might result in a higher interest from their senior people and a greater determination to maintain standards, or that all the mistakes would be made on our work and that the learning would then be put to use on future arrangements with our competitors and others.

'What I would like as an outcome from this meeting is an indication of your preliminary thoughts on the offer – which I have circulated to you all – so that Mrs Hoskins and I can have a meeting with them and probe this further. I would emphasise that we have at present no commitment whatsoever even to talk to them about this. We need to identify first whether the idea is worth pursuing and, if some further investigation is required, to set a pattern for it. So, let me start with the first item on the agenda...'

Establishing a Framework

'Good morning. I am delighted that you and your colleagues could come in and meet us today. You have seen the outline of what is required for the bid and I believe that we have sent you some information about our company ... Good. That should give you a very general view of what we do and don't do. Would you like me to start by setting out our position and how we see things moving forward? ... Right.

'We see ourselves as very much in line for all of the plant supply side of this contract and would be keen to undertake the installation and after-sales maintenance. We are not so well known for the upfront feasibility work and the financial analysis. We are of the view that to raise the funding for the project, we need to have an organisation like yours on board. We would certainly seem to be world-beaters if we could find such a route. However, while I understand that you are happy in principle to join with us, I believe that you have a number of reservations, may I call them reservations? Indeed, so have we.

'My proposal is that we exchange information on skills and experience here in our head offices and each of us sends one senior person to meet representatives of the Thai government and the World Bank and decide whether we wish to be involved in putting together a joint bid ...'

The Single Deal

'We are of the view that our air conditioning was never really adequate from the start. We have been advised that there is nothing we can sensibly do to pursue the original designers or suppliers and will just have to sort it out ourselves. As your company provided the original chiller units to the system – and we are quite satisfied that there is nothing wrong with them – we would like to upgrade them when we beef up the rest of the system.'

'This is quite a tricky one but we do have the technical skills to handle it. I will arrange for one of our technicians to call and run some tests. He will be able to assess how much more capacity you will need and how it might be built in to the present system. We may not be able to use the present chiller but have to replace it with a bigger one.'

'As you wish. I am looking at a number of options and you must decide whether you can upgrade or replace. My approach will depend on how the others will handle the problem and the complexity, quality and cost of their proposals.'

The Long-Term Relationship

'I'm pleased that we could visit you today. The exchanges that have taken place so far indicate that we might be able to do a deal but there are some points that we still need to agree.'

'Well, thank you for coming. In view of the number of cross-channel trips that your people will be making, we would very much like to become your preferred service provider. Of course, we have to be aware of our own cost base and many other factors, but you will already appreciate our determination to offer the best terms over-all. Would you like to work through the points that you have on your agenda?'

'Yes, thank you. We certainly appreciate your expressions of interest and they have been clear throughout the initial discussions. Base discounts against your standard tariffs have been agreed between our teams and I do not intend to revisit those. We must, however, have a formula that protects us in the event that your fare tariffs go up more than those of your competitors. I am thinking of something which relates our costs to the lowest fares offered on the route, rather than to those your company charges.'

'Oh, dear me, no. That would open us up to completely unknown discounts and place our fare tariffs in the hands of our competitors. But I do recognise your genuine concerns in this. I have some ideas that may be of interest to you to overcome this and which might enable a longer-term contract to be agreed ...'

NEEDS, WANTS, DESIRES

Discussing objectives in the abstract is useful but does not enable the negotiator to have a clear framework within which to develop these objectives. Such a framework may be defined by reference to the possible outcomes from the negotiation and the needs, wants and desires that one views as applying to the challenge in hand. These definitions provide the parameters within which the negotiation will take place, as represented by Figure 3.2.

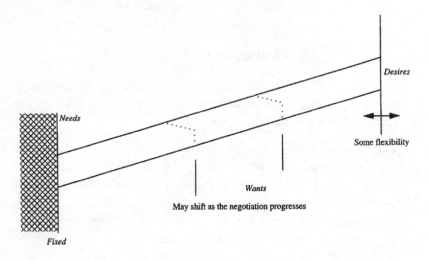

Figure 3.2 Needs, wants and desires.

Needs

Needs represent the minimum possible set of achievements that you must expect to gain from this negotiation. If you are unable to achieve these, then you should certainly pull out and not seek a deal at all. Needs have to be expressed in relation to each single aspect that has been identified as possibly arising in the negotiation and, if other aspects become part of the process, needs must be defined for them as well. Thus, in every respect there is a need defined, below which the negotiator will not go.

The question that is often posed is whether any single need can be varied when unexpected benefit has been obtained on another

issue. This should not be possible if the need has been determined accurately in the first place. If this need clearly is the minimum on that particular aspect, then it cannot be varied.

But elsewhere has been given the message that there are no golden rules, so perhaps it is inappropriate to see this definition of needs as rigid, as a golden rule that can never be broken. There can of course be occasions when a need can be overturned and when other factors can require us to set aside a position that was taken earlier in the negotiation, and possibly well before many of the factors were clear.

The objection to ever changing a need must be seen in the context of flexibility and particularly of the dynamic nature of negotiations. It can often be impossible to retain all of the needs which were defined at the earliest stage of a negotiation but, equally, such defined needs should be defended and only be thrown out once there is a very strong, even overwhelming, case for rejecting them.

If one is managing negotiators, the extent to which these needs have been defined clearly, and on a strong basis of evidence and fact, is something that has to be examined with care. If the negotiators have not obtained a clear picture of the needs from that specific exchange, then you probably have the wrong people doing the job and should seek to give significant guidance prior to allowing them to face the opposition.

Wants

Wants represent the reasonable position that should be achieved as a result of good, positive, well prepared negotiation. Achieving your wants will give you a good outcome from the deal and deliver to your organisation what was required. They should represent a good balance between the options that will be negotiated and one of the core problems in setting them is to examine the optimum balance and achieve it. We saw that needs were absolute – but with a small amount of flexibility to change them under extreme circumstances – but wants may be pitched within a range and be acceptable. However, if a range can be avoided in order that everyone on your team has the same view of the wants, then it should be.

The problem with defining a range, or a bracket into which the wants should fall, is that different people will then perceive these wants differently. One group will assume that the most advantageous end of the range is the true want while others will identify that they can quite readily accept a solution that lies towards the lesser end. If it is not possible to decide on single statements of want for each topic to be covered, then the negotiating team should return to their preparation and develop their ideas further. If a single point is still not possible, all those involved in the negotiation should understand the range and the reasons for it.

Desires

Desires represent the position to which I might aspire if my side of the negotiation is thoroughly prepared, presented competently, argued with excellence and pursued with such flexibility and courage as to overwhelm the opposition, who themselves had achieved none of this substance in their work. Desires thus represent positions which I do not seriously expect to achieve but would be delighted if I could.

What then is the purpose of defining these desires? The principal reason is that it forces the negotiator to consider the ultimate point to which the negotiation might be pressed and the degree to which there might be flexibility on the part of the opponents. If the distance between the wants and the desires is substantial, there may well be something wrong with the target setting approach. Perhaps then the wants should move into a rather more aggressive and demanding position; but perhaps the view of the desires is far from reality.

In truth, it is the setting of the desires position that provides the most value, rather than trying to negotiate towards it. If the successful negotiator really is gaining significantly more ground than expected, the critical thing is to ensure that such gain is on the issues which are important and in such a balance as to ensure that the benefits can be realised. An understanding of the desires will be valuable, but the thought process which went into identifying those desires can perhaps contribute at least as much as the definition of the desires themselves.

Needs

The worst position to which I am willing to be pushed and which I will accept. If I cannot achieve this position, I will cease to negotiate.

Wants

The position which I believe to represent a reasonable expression of my expectations from this negotiation and which I fully expect to achieve if I handle it correctly and with due skill.

Desires

The position which I hope to achieve if everything I have not thought of falls in my favour, if I handle my side of the negotiation with exceptional skill and the other side fails to perform adequately.

For each of the elements of the proposed deal, no matter how large or small they might appear to be at an early stage in the negotiation process, a *need*, *want* and *desire* position must be established. Once the aspects have been dealt with individually, the set should then be examined to ensure overall coherence and consistency. It may be necessary to run through the process of target-setting of these needs, wants and desires for the first time and then review them to ensure that they do indeed have coherence. The process is worth a significant amount of your preparation time since it sets the parameters within which you expect to negotiate and helps identify what truly are the objectives that your organisation should be seeking from the deal which is to be struck.

During a major negotiation, there is often value in setting aside time to carry out a complete review of these needs, wants and desires. As the negotiation has progressed, your team will have learned more and will probably wish to redefine their positions. If this results in realistic repositioning of the wants position first and foremost, there can be no objection to it. If on the other hand it gives rise to a serious challenge to the position earlier defined by the needs and a drive to push the targets downwards, then the team leader or the manager should have concern.

It is then necessary to ask a series of key questions:

○ Have team members become so embroiled that they are seeking any deal rather than the right one?

○ Have they lost on some significant points and are now seeking to keep their wants position at a logical distance between their needs and desires by moving their needs down the scale?

○ How strong is the opponents' case and how powerful their arguments? Has my team been convinced incorrectly of their own position in relation to that of their opponents?

○ Were the original targets set appropriately or can they quite correctly be moved at this stage and still have the potential of yielding a reasonable outcome?

○ Are we in such a poor position and so much in need of this deal that we really have no choice and truly do have to revise all our expectations downwards and still try to do the best deal?

○ Have we reached the point where someone has to say that there is no deal to be made out of this negotiation and that we should withdraw and live to fight another issue on another day?

The setting, review, revision and confirming of needs, wants and desires is a very powerful system of tools available to the negotiator. As with any other tool, usage requires training, skill and practice, but it also requires external appraisal to ensure that the user is aware of what is still to be learned and improved upon.

We will return many times in this book to this theme because it is these needs, wants and desires that form the very basis of what we are negotiating, how we will go about negotiating it, and the information we will need to do so. Most good writers and lecturers approach negotiation from this angle, although there are many ways of defining these parameters. Whatever they are called, it is of great significance to the outcome of a negotiation for the parameters to be fully understood by the individual negotiator or the team.

It will, then, be clear that the needs, wants and desires parameters cannot be defined for a negotiator. It is unreasonable to expect anyone to go forward to try to do a deal with only these factors in mind and no knowledge of how or why they were decided upon. If there is a need to move around within the parameters in order to obtain a deal that is overall better from your own viewpoint, quite regardless of what your opponent is seeking, then the negotiator upon whom such parameters have been imposed is unable to manoeuvre appropriately.

Furthermore, when the opponent is seemingly locked on a specific point and cannot find movement, the negotiator must have opportunities to help with movement elsewhere (as long as the other side was *genuinely* stuck on a point). Thus, the negotiator should develop, or be a major influence in developing, the needs, wants and desires that will form the backbone of the negotiation and must fully understand them and believe them to be appropriate. If that is not the case, either the parameters are wrong, or the negotiator is.

ARE YOU REALLY NEGOTIATING?

It is not unusual to hear people say that they have not started negotiations but are meeting the other side to sort out some initial points, obtain clarification of others and seek information about the deal that is being considered. If they truly do feel that they are not at that time *really* negotiating, they need to be pulled back and invited to take negotiation lessons. As soon as you start any dealings with parties with whom you might reach agreement and do commercial deals, you are negotiating. Right from the start, both you and they will be seeking information that may be of value later, you are seeking to understand the other side's economic position in the markets in which you operate, and you are looking for openings that will give you further understanding of their business in general.

Assume, therefore, that every meeting is a negotiation. But not every session needs to comprise the sort of intensive cut and thrust that can occur when two parties are trying to squeeze out the last ounces from a deal that has largely been done. Many early sessions may be much more relaxed, but you should still ensure that you do not give away information, either hard or soft, that you would not have divulged at a more formal point in a negotiation.

On this point, it is interesting to try to write down in around 10 minutes as many reasons as you can as to why salespeople seem keen to take so many buyers and other business contacts out to lunch.

Lunch Before Negotiations

'Hello, may I speak to Mrs Stubbs, please? It's Belinda Harvey of Dynamic Services speaking... Ah, yes, hello, just a quick call. I'm coming to your place next Wednesday to talk over some thoughts prior to taking this long-term contract thing forward. As we are due to meet at 2 o'clock, I wondered if we might have some lunch first. I could arrange somewhere local to you and reasonably quick. You might like to bring along a couple of colleagues, you know, just to stop us talking business all through lunch. Wouldn't want to spoil the lunch would we?... Ah, excellent.... I can get to know them at the same time... See you at 12.30 then... Splendid... Bye.'

4

The win-win concept

Let me not to the marriage of true minds
Admit impediments.

William Shakespeare, *Sonnets*, 116.

Much is talked about how all successful negotiations must have concluded with win-win situations, otherwise they would not have been successful. This means that both sides feel that the outcome represented a win for them. Indeed there are those who will argue that a negotiation is successful *if and only if* it results in win-win.

From the viewpoint of each party, it would be possible to take the view that either one would have broken off the discussion if they did not feel that adequate terms could be agreed so that a win could be claimed. After all, a win in a negotiation does not require the other party to have been beaten, merely to have yielded enough so that at least your needs have been achieved, and hopefully some of your wants as well.

We will look at these issues in this chapter and examine just what the significance of win-win is to the negotiator and how it might impact upon the negotiator's thinking at all stages. By the end of the chapter enough of the issues will have been examined for three questions to be answered. These are:

○ Should all negotiations result in win-win?

○ Should negotiators be seeking win-win from the outset?

○ Can you assume that your opponent is seeking win-win?

It is worth examining these three questions very closely because much that is said and written about win-win can be very misleading.

WINNING FOR YOUR OWN SIDE

When in doubt, win the trick.

Edmond Hoyle, Hoyle's Games – *Whist*,
'Twenty-four Short Rules for Learners'.

Before diving headlong into the topic of winning for your own side, let us examine the idea as it applies to sport – thereby continuing the useful analogy which we have used previously.

There may be a number of situations in sport where you do not set out to win. It is worthwhile looking at these first and then seeing whether they have any significance to us in considering our approach to negotiating. A win may not be sought in a number of scenarios, for example:

○ Father to 8-year-old son: 'Race you to the top of the hill.'

○ 'As long as I can finish this 800 metres in the first four, I go through into the next round.'

○ 'If we win this last match, we play Brazil in the quarter finals; if we lose or draw, we still go through but play Malta.'

○ 'With the home win behind us and that away goal, even losing by one goal sends us through safely into the next round.'

○ 'I don't want to win and beat my best friend. He has trained so hard for this.'

We can see immediately that the first picture has no realistic parallel in commercial negotiating. It would be absurd to pretend to be negotiating while all the time helping the other side to win. Whilst it may be possible to conjure up some hypothetical situations, we can accept that they are unlikely to arise in practice. If you ever get near to such a position, there are better ways to deal with it than by the pretence of negotiation.

The next three cases, however, do have parallels in the field of negotiation. There will be many times in the negotiator's life when it is not necessary to pursue the immediate and absolute win. Just as the examples give us indications of how to retain the chance to win overall without perhaps winning this round, we can choose to do the same in the commercial field. One will win what is needed for the time being and retain the option to win some more later. Or one might only fight on a certain front and be content for the time being to win that section only.

The major difference here between negotiating and sport is that the negotiator will rarely want to allow his opponent to win a round if it can be avoided. Yes, there may be occasions when to lose on a selected element could be to your longer-term advantage, but there is danger in giving too much away on such occasions. In the sporting analogy, perhaps one should only let one's opponents have a draw since permitting them to win generally goes against everything that keen and determined sportspeople stand for.

Generally speaking, the same position applies in sport as in commercial negotiating. In fact it is much the same as the position that has to be taken up in times of war:

We are not interested in the possibilities of defeat.

Queen Victoria, to A. J. Balfour, December 1899.

We must always be seeking a win for our own side, otherwise we may stumble to a draw or, even worse, defeat. The only way to ensure a win is to seek one.

We can see therefore that the first part of the expression 'win-win' – that is, that we should be determined to win – is easy to understand. It is why we thought we were negotiating. We thought our objective was to win. And so it is.

WINNING FOR THE OTHER SIDE

Faint heart never won fair lady!
Nothing venture, nothing win ...

Sir William Schwenck Gilbert, *Iolanthe*.

Who, then, is to ensure that the other side has the most chance of winning? Quite obviously it must be the other side. Their team will be – or should be – fully trained to take you on, to score as many or more off you as you will off them. Their key objective will be the same as yours – they will set out to win and, if you accept the deal that they feel they have won, that is your concern and not theirs.

You have to assume that it is the objective of your opponents to win whatever they can for themselves. Just as it would be strange for you to be trying to win for them, it will be odd if they are trying to win for you.

"Greetings Garth. Why not pop around the cave one evening to toss around some ideas?"

WHOSE JOB IS WIN-WIN?

Then who should be going into the fray with the idea that both sides must win by the time the final whistle blows? Clearly nobody should. Whoever does will be more likely to come out at best in the draw-win situation and almost certainly they will find that it is lose-win.

When going into a negotiation, you must have as your priority to obtain all of your wants and as many of your desires as you can. You must fight as hard and as skilfully as you can and gain as much commercial advantage for your organisation as is possible. Your opponents will equally have their own agenda of needs, wants and desires which may or may not match yours. If you are good at what you are doing, you will gradually come to form a picture of these sets of targets. If you are successful in your work, you will get to know their needs and their wants; if you are less successful, you will come to recognise their wants and some of their desires.

But can it ever be your job as a negotiator to set up a win-win position? Yes, it can, but rarely.

We Do Not Win Unless They Do

'I think we could have a problem with this body-shop deal. I cannot see how they can make any money on our repairs and new vehicle livery work. Their prices are just too low and the deliveries and turnround times they are offering are so short that they will have to work hours of overtime and most weekends. That will inflate their prices no end. Either that or they will give us back rubbish and we will have to spend hours of time and vast sums to get it all put right.'

'Yes, I agree. I was rather surprised when they put in their bid and then again when they offered to knock it down a bit if they were not lowest. It's not that they are technically incompetent, it's just that the owner has little idea of commercial realities. The problem is that he currently does first-class work and is just round the corner. We've got to replace that cowboy outfit that we have at the moment.'

'OK. Let's try and do a deal with him. We'll pay the rates that he is asking but monitor his finances carefully. We will be taking around 70 per cent of his capacity and he's not working for any of our competitors. We'll do the whole thing on an open-book basis and give him a bit of help with his accounting. If he really is losing money, we will pay a bit more – we have a margin in hand before we reach the cost of the next quote. That way we get a quality service cheap, he doesn't have to pay more for clerical staff, we can ensure that he makes a reasonable profit and he will need us so much he will have to do the job properly. What do you think?'

'I agree completely. But I do think I'm going to have a very surprised contractor in my office this afternoon!'

WHY TALK OF WIN-WIN?

The main significance of the expression itself is to commentators on the subject of negotiation, rather than to negotiators themselves. Rarely will you hear experienced negotiators use the expression as an indication of their *objectives*. When one has seen a competently managed negotiation in practice, and studied and analysed the outcome, it is interesting to assess the extent to which the result was a win-win scenario. In most cases this will have been the outcome.

Two reasonably capable negotiators against each other, each having at least some idea of their needs, wants and desires, will usually come to a position where each has retained enough to have felt that the negotiation has been 'won' (see Figure 4.1).

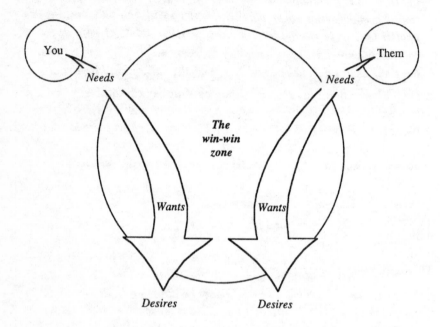

Figure 4.1 The win-win zone.

This does not mean that each party feels that it came out with a far better deal than the other side, but that each gained or held on to enough ground to achieve an acceptable outcome. The observer might feel that one party did considerably better than the other but, if both found the deal to be even marginally above the threshold level, then it may be considered a win-win scenario.

The concept, then, has more application to observers and teachers trying to draw out messages than to the individual negotiator. There is a need when involved in a negotiation to consider whether the position might arise whereby the terms on offer are unlikely to be acceptable to the other side and whether that matters to you. If it does, then you have to give a little to bring them back on board and present them with an outcome that is marginally above the level of their defined needs.

PARTNERING

Partnering is a recent term for what many have regarded as tradi-tional good practice in procurement. The philosophy of partnering applies to a wide range of practical situations, but its essence is co-operation and shared responsibility between supplier and purchaser for their mutual benefit. The adversarial relationship between the parties to a supply or services contract is replaced by a common aim based on mutual trust to produce an optimum final outcome from which both parties can benefit.

Quality Through Competition in Defence, Paper by the Market Testing Organisation, Ministry of Defence, 1994.

Many deals which are being done today reflect the concept that business is assisted by having long-term commercial arrangements which are satisfactory to both parties, rather than a series of short-term deals covering much the same range of buyer and seller needs. This is not the place to consider whether partnering in any given set of circumstances might be appropriate, but it is worthwhile examin-ing how the concept might change our approach to negotiation.

It is the Japanese motor industry that seems to be credited by most observers and commentators with having conceived and devel-oped the idea of partnering. Retailers in Europe have claimed that they have been pursuing such ideas for many years, and a number of other industries around the world also argue that it is no more and no less than they have practised as a matter of course. Whoever invented the idea is, perhaps, less important than the wide agreement that it can yield substantial benefits for many economic sectors.

The concept requires you to make far longer-term arrangements with your trading partners than you had previously, recognising that your interests and theirs are better served by knowing about the commercial nature of deals over the long term. Both supply and demand can be assured – depending on which side you are – and the economic basis of your business can be evaluated to enable sensible decisions to be taken.

In broad terms, the advantages and disadvantages of partnering may be summed up as in Table 4.1. The views are expressed from the standpoint of the buyers of a range of goods essential for their own organisation's products.

Table 4.1 Partnering – for and against

Advantages	*Disadvantages*
○ You will have consistency in terms of specification and quality.	
	○ You are locked in to market conditions, even when they change to your advantage.
○ Lower costs arise for tendering and negotiation over the life of the deal.	
	○ Contact with prices and qualities in the general market-place can be lost.
○ A major aspect of your own operating cost base is known.	
	○ There is a risk that a better possible deal emerges after the contract is signed.
○ Complaints to the supplier may be treated more sympathetically and quickly.	
	○ If your market declines, you may have a buying commitment you cannot finance.
○ The supplier can invest in better facilities with more confidence.	
	○ Your supplier may not perform, but the contract is in place for a long time.
○ People can be properly trained to handle the specific incoming products.	
	○ Your skills in marketing and selling may diminish through lack of use.
○ Operational controls such as just-in-time planning will be easier to install.	

It will be seen that, not only are there fewer disadvantages, but some are reasonably easy to overcome. You might choose, for example, to:

○ negotiate a deal linked to market conditions, allowing prices to both rise and fall within certain bands;

○ link your supplier's deliveries to the ultimate demand for your own products;

○ put in place a number of measures to ensure good liaison on key matters so that any deterioration in service can be identified and checked at a very early stage;

○ ensure that, as the supply line is critical to both of you, the most senior people on each side are aware of it and positively wish to resolve difficulties quickly.

We must examine whether the negotiation of a partnering deal would be expected to run any differently from that for a once-off deal. It might be expected that the strong desire to set up a long-term relationship, drawing on common interest and goodwill, would make such negotiation somewhat easier. That is not, in fact, what happens in practice.

We have seen that a partnering arrangement can be of the utmost significance to both of the parties involved and it is therefore critical that each party achieves terms that are satisfactory, that enable them to work within the arrangement, that provide them with adequate cash flow, profit or whatever other driver is crucial to them, and that they will not have other competitive pressures that will prevent delivery on this contract. It will also be of great importance to both parties to ensure that the fine detail is thoroughly negotiated since even relatively small differences in the terms could generate major impacts over the life of the contract.

Therefore, even though there may be more *goodwill* on both sides, the terms are likely to be argued over as fiercely as on a once-off deal. Both parties will put their very best negotiators into the arena and both will be determined to ensure that they obtain totally satisfactory deals. The argument that partnering requires a quite different type of negotiation in principle does not seem to be borne out in practice. All of the normal requirements of negotiation are in place, but there is a sharper edge to each of the factors being negotiated because of their added importance and long-term impact on both sides.

Is this to say, then, that there is absolutely no difference between partnering and once-off negotiations? No, it is not. There are differences, but they are not of great magnitude. They are principally that, in negotiating a partnering deal, you are likely to find:

○ fewer tricks pulled by both parties;

○ more openness and frankness about each party's requirements;

○ each knows quite a lot about the other's markets and flexibility;

○ a genuine will to do business rather than to just test the water;

○ better qualities of negotiating skill on each side;

○ higher management levels involved on both sides.

In taking on board the lessons from this book, these nuances will need to be borne in mind. Any differences in approach should certainly be identified during the preparation process and during the setting and confirmation of your side's needs, wants and desires. They will be reinforced when you are setting your strategy and defining the tactics and techniques that you will use.

We will not, therefore, examine the partnering concept too much during the remaining chapters, except to identify occasionally where the approach may have an appreciable impact on certain of the topics under discussion.

THE SCENARIO OPTIONS

Although there are in theory a number of options and combinations of win, lose and draw as they might apply to two opposed negotiators, the most common is, for reasons described above, the win-win. But win-lose can also occur, and quite often does. It is convenient to take some examples to illustrate all of the patterns that can emerge in this respect and these are given in the boxes which follow.

Win-Win

The Travel Service

When British Telecom (BT) were looking to reduce the costs of making travel arrangements for their employees, they invited tenders from a number of reputable travel agents. After evaluating the tenders, they selected Hogg Robinson (Travel) Ltd as their preferred supplier, subject to satisfactory contract negotiations.

Amongst other factors for discussion, they were looking for cost reductions beyond those to be gained within the terms of the tender and had some concerns about the number of locations from which the service would be provided.

In their turn, Hogg Robinson had to face issues relating to recruiting and training the extra staff, accommodating them, and providing the voice and computer communication links essential to their efficient and effective working.

The two companies eventually agreed that surplus BT premises could be used by the agent, that BT would guarantee to supply the lines needed into those facilities and that enough of the reduction in charges that had been sought by BT could be offered by Hogg Robinson.

Overall, both companies achieved their objectives and sufficient of their wants and desires for a win-win deal to be done.

The Job Offer

'I am delighted that you are able to join me today and meet Mr Cager again. Our objective is to agree the terms on which you would take up the Distribution Manager's post. We have cleared most of the terms of the appointment but I believe that you still have some concerns about the formal offer letter we have sent you.'

'Yes. It did seem the best approach to take these up with you and Mr Cager direct rather than continue through letters. As you know, I am happy with the salary and most other terms but the profit-share is only about half what I am seeking. The job will have a major impact on profitability. And I understood that there would be a directorship. There is no mention of that in the offer letter.'

'*We could put the profit-related element on a sliding scale so that you would have a larger bonus if they went up more than we expect. I have drafted out this note which explains the option. See what you think... On the directorship question, I will not give a commitment at this time. That will follow on the heels of success. After all, we won't want to lose you if you prove to be as good as we expect!*'

'This bonus approach looks much more attractive and it is in line with what I was seeking. I think we have a deal.'

Win-Lose

The Gypsy at the Door

Knock ... knock.

'*Good afternoon ma'am. I'm travelling with my family and these are some of my children. We have stopped in your area to bring you luck. I can offer you this lucky heather or some of these lovely hankies. Or I can tell your fortune and how you can stop any of life's nasty things happening to you.*'

'No thank you. Nothing thank you.'

'*Now you can't just say that and turn me and my kids away with nothing, can you? We've come to make sure you don't have any bad luck and you don't want to know. I'm sure that just a sprig of heather from the magic hills is just what you need.*'

'Oh, all right then. How much do you want for it?'

'*Whatever you feel you can afford to buy yourself some good luck and avoid all the curses of modern living.*'

'Here's a pound. No I don't want the heather.'

'*There you are, you three. Step forward and take your pounds from the nice lady.*'

So, a clear case of win-lose. The gypsy clearly gained. She got what she went for and lost nothing. The householder did not want the gypsy on her doorstep in the first place so she gained nothing. She lost £3 and certainly fell far short of what she would have defined as her needs.

One out – All out

Knock ... knock.

'Oh it's you. I'm busy. What do you want? Can't it wait?'

'I'm afraid not. My colleagues and I are very angry. We are just not happy to have one of us thrown out like that. And to accuse him of stealing ...'

'He was taking money from the till. And he stole videos and had them in his house. Of course he was stealing.'

'He had perfectly valid reasons for both those things. The videos came back after the store was locked and he was taking his expenses from the till. He would have put his receipts in later.'

'He's sacked and he stays sacked. That's the end of it.'

'Either he comes back and you arrange an independent investigation or we close the place right now until you do. And we'll get the regional manager here as well.'

'I can find plenty of other people to work here. There are thousands out there who would scab on you without turning a hair.'

'We wanted to be reasonable, but if that is your last word, consider yourself closed.'

'Just a minute. Don't be so silly. Nobody liked him anyway. I'm sure we can sort something out. OK, he comes back and I forget all about it this time ...'

Lose-Lose

Bailiffs at the Door

'Hello, we know you're in there. It's the bailiffs. You knew we were coming. Open the door.'

'I won't. Go away. You're not taking anything of mine.'

'*Don't be so stupid. We're only doing our job. We don't like this any more than you do.*'

'Well don't do it then. Just clear off and say you couldn't get in.'

'*Can't do that. We're going to get in somehow. If you won't open the door, we'll break it down.*'

'It's barred. And so are the windows. It'll take you hours to get in. While you are at it I'll smash everything. Nobody will get my stuff.'

'*OK lads, there's the door ...*'

Mr Five Per Cent

'*Right, we've talked for weeks about this. Five per cent consolidated on basic. And that sweeps up all the other details we've been discussing. It's all we can afford.*'

'Whoa. We were near to agreement. Now you want to go back-wards. Our members are expecting a number of things from this deal. Restructuring, consolidation, regrading, productivity payments ...'

'*Tough. That's my final offer. None of this rubbish. You are just trying to squeeze out more than you're entitled to. I'm on to you.*'

'We won't be able to keep the guys in the shop if you do that. They will want a lot more to come back after walking out. And you'll lose production and that overseas order.'

'*Don't try to blackmail me. Get out. There's the door ...*'

IN SUMMARY

To pull all of this together, it is appropriate to look back at the three questions that were posed earlier in this chapter:

O Should all negotiations result in win-win?

O Should negotiators be seeking win-win from the outset?

O Can you assume that your opponent is seeking win-win?

Clearly, the answer to the first question is that not all negotiations will result in win-win, nor should they be expected to. Two examples have been given which did not achieve win-win and there could be many more. The desperate supplier who has to concede on his needs simply to grab an order to stay in business cannot be considered – except by the greatest stretch of the imagination – to be in a winning position. The manager who has no cards to play in avoiding industrial action cannot be considered to be in a winning position. And the customer who makes no purchase because the terms on offer were not good enough has not won anything. The answer to the first question is, therefore:

O No, not all negotiations have to result in win-win.

With regard to the second question, if a negotiator sets out to achieve win-win, then much of the purpose of the negotiation has largely been conceded from the outset. Set out to achieve win for your side and assume that the other side is doing the same. Never worry about achieving a win situation for them but look after your own interests and ensure that your side of the deal is as satisfactory as you can make it. Although you should not be seeking win-win positively, you should ensure that your opponent is likely to be able to deliver on his side of the bargain. If you have won too much ground, you may feel pleased with yourself initially, but disappointed when the deal is declined or the other party to it fails subsequently. So, the answer to the second question must be:

O No, never set out to achieve win-win. Simply seek win.

Dealing with the third question is equally as easy. Quite simply, you must assume that your opponent has little regard for your position and is seeking simply to win on his own account. If that is not the case, why is he negotiating at all? Why not simply tell you what terms would be acceptable and then take them if they are on offer or decline if they are not? No, the whole purpose of negotiation is to squeeze out that little bit extra – and that does not seem like the action of someone who is trying to help *you* win. As things progress, maybe you will begin to feel that you were wrong and not doing justice to this fine person sitting opposite you. But it is better to be safe than sorry. The answer to the third question is, therefore:

O No, assume that your opponent is entirely self-centred, until proven otherwise.

To close this chapter, it is worth looking at a sensible tenet that applies to many aspects of business and quite certainly to the art and science of negotiation. Always remember: a deal which is good for you but not good enough for the other side will probably come back to haunt you before it is over. It is likely to cause you problems that you did not want, and certainly will not have envisaged. Poor deals will hinder you in achieving your own objectives; good deals will help you to achieve them. And always remember that you may need to do business with the same people again some time.

You have to keep on doing business in your own area and you keep coming across the same people. They will remember you from last time and that will affect how they deal with you.

Barry Hubbard, Business Development Manager,
Northumberland TEC.

5

The preparation stage

Be Prepared.

Motto of the Scout Association.

Nam et ipsa scientia potestas est.
(Knowledge itself is power.)

Francis Bacon, *Of Heresies.*

THE PREPARATION PROCESS

In negotiating, knowledge is indeed power. Knowledge gives you a picture of where to pitch your needs, wants and desires and of how you might reach them. It then gives you the power to drive the negotiating process in the direction you choose towards an outcome on which you have decided.

Thorough preparation is essential to give you this power, but it is also essential for you to be able to demonstrate to your colleagues why your preferred route is the most appropriate and why your selection of the person or people to do the negotiating is correct. Preparation covers five main areas in negotiation. These are:

O establishing the overall targets;

O collecting and analysing information;

O defining the strategy to be adopted;

O selecting the tactics to be employed;

O identifying the skills needed.

This chapter will deal with the first two of these topics, while later chapters will address the remaining issues.

It is useful to consider when you are preparing for a negotiation that you are building yourself a platform from which to discuss, debate and bargain. But it is not one simple platform, it is a set of such positions defined by your needs, wants and desires. This concept is useful because it conjures up a pictorial image of your position. You are there both to defend your platform against aggressors and to assist those who are more friendly to move nearer to your platform and then up on to it. Of course, your platform must not be considered as fixed – it can take up a position anywhere between your needs and your desires, but preferably as near to your desires as possible. You will be adjusting the height and accessibility of your platform throughout the negotiation to make it easier or more difficult for the other side to climb aboard. And, of course, you will even be tilting the platform a bit from time to time just to show your opponent how pleasant it would be to be on there with you and doing business.

This concept of a platform is all very well until you consider that both sides in the negotiation have been building very much the same thing, but some distance apart from each other. If you simply sit tight on your own platforms, there will never be a deal. You must both therefore be making moves to bring those platforms closer together so that it is a simple matter for either of you to move to the other's platform, or for them to merge into one. The happiest outcome will usually be that there is no discernable difference between your positions at the end as you have both compromised to some degree – although, of course, your objective in negotiating is to win more compromise from the other side than you will be yielding yourself!

Returning, then, to the detailed issues of preparation, it will be noted that there has been no specific reference to the fact that a key element for every negotiator is to attempt to identify as accurately as possible the likely platform from which the other side is coming and the way in which they will set about handling their end of the negotiation. We will look at this as we go through, since it has relevance to a number of sections in differing degrees.

It is also important to recognise that the process of preparation is iterative. Whilst you can certainly set yourself targets at the outset, you will only come to know if they are reasonable once you have obtained information and examined such issues as your possible strategies and those likely to be adopted by your opponents. Thus, you may work in a disciplined way through the first three steps and become increasingly uncomfortable about just how to handle this particular negotiation. You then need to jump back to the start and examine just what you are seeking from the process upon which you are about to embark. You perhaps need to ask yourself a series of questions of the type:

O Have I assessed correctly the framework within which I am negotiating?

O Can I really take this in one step, or do I need to take on less in the first instance?

O If I cannot see a route to achieving my targets, do I in reality have a chance of getting to them?

O Are the heights to which we are seeking to aspire actually beyond us?

O Have I properly understood what I am being asked to do?

O Am I, in fact, the best person to be handling this in all the circumstances?

Perhaps you will end up back at the point which you had reached earlier and conclude that in this negotiation you can find no route to putting yourself into a winning position, that the cards which you hold are not in fact strong enough to give you the game. If that is the case, and there is no choice but to continue, at least you have a realistic picture of your position and can select your strategy and tactics so that they give you the best chance available of achieving your targets – even if that chance is still not particularly good.

In the great majority of cases, going back through the loop once you have begun to identify weaknesses, problems or high hurdles will enhance your understanding of the process upon which you are embarking and your prospects of achieving a satisfactory outcome.

Before moving on to the question of targets, we will first take a wide look at the generic objectives which you have in following a negotiating process. This will give us a number of useful pointers as to what we should prepare and how we should go about it.

Well, I think you have to have really good preparation, you've got to really know what you want to do, what you're out there to achieve.

Patsy Bloom, Chief Executive, *Pet Plan Insurance.*

OBJECTIVES RESTATED

In order to ascertain why we are preparing and what, let us revisit briefly our objectives. We examined these in a previous chapter but will look at them in a somewhat different way and from this develop our approach to preparation.

We will assume that you have carefully examined your position and interests and defined your needs, wants and desires. Is there anything else you need to do? Indeed there is. You must clarify your position against five key objectives. We will look at them one by one.

The first objective in negotiation is to ensure that all the topics that you wish to have discussed are covered and dealt with to your satisfaction.

You must therefore know the topics you wish to cover, must have identified how they interact with each other and why you want them brought into the discussion. This is not quite as easy as it sounds. You may know, for example, that certain topics have to be covered but that your position on them is likely to be weak or that these topics will expose other areas which you do not wish to have debated. Nevertheless, if you know that they have to be covered, you must ensure that they are brought in.

The whole reason for identifying all of the issues which you wish to have covered is so that you will prepare on all of them. That way, you can take a positive line on everything, be thoroughly briefed and have a clear picture of your flexibility, the risks you face and your needs, wants and desires.

This leads us directly on to the second objective, which also relates directly to both your preparation for and management of the negotiation process:

The second objective in negotiating is to ensure either that those points which you do not wish to have raised are not raised or, if they are, that you can suitably counter them.

To achieve this you must have identified the topics which you wish to avoid equally as well as you identified those you wish to include. There may be a number of points that you prefer to see excluded from the discussion, for example:

○ linking a deal to a longer-term relationship;

○ a poor history of service on your organisation's part;

○ reasons for failing to achieve satisfactory terms in the past;

○ a change in your organisation that could be considered as adverse;

○ a need to subcontract that you do not wish to admit.

The Negotiating Ostrich

'Thank goodness we were able to meet with enough time to go through these points thoroughly and comprehensively. I think that clears up all the areas that we feel are our strengths and we have sorted out who will present and argue each one. Now I'd like to look at the other side of the coin and at our opponent's possible arguments ...'

'What do you mean? Our job is to worry about our arguments, not about theirs. We want to go into this positively. I'm not having you lot even thinking about the things we don't want talked about.'

'I can't agree with that. What if they raise the fact that on the previous occasion we supplied a type 483G it failed as soon as it was powered up?'

'Tell them it was someone else's fault.'

'And what if they ask about press reports of our top technical people leaving and going to work for competitors?'

'Tell them they're rubbish.'

'And what if they ask about the factory being demolished by fire?'

'Tell them it didn't happen.'

'And what if ...'

'Look here. I want people on my team who think positively. Not wets who just want to grovel around in excuses. Hit 'em hard with what we want to tell 'em. Sell, sell, sell.'

'But we really do have sensible and credible counters to ...'

'Right, I warned you, you're off the team. Now, anyone else who thinks negative?'

There could be many more such circumstances, which will depend on the topics up for negotiation and your own position in relation to them.

How, then, can you ensure that these will not be raised? Clearly, you cannot. But you can find ways to reduce the prospect of them being raised and be prepared for dealing with them if they are. But you will only satisfy this objective if you have first identified the topics that represent danger to you.

Once you have identified all of the danger areas, you need to do two things. These are:

O to identify ways to avoid the undesirable issues being raised;

O to have ready counters for them if they are.

Later sections in this and subsequent chapters will be examining how you can achieve this second objective.

In skating over thin ice, our safety is in our speed.

Ralph Waldo Emerson, *Prudence*.

Having now ascertained just what you do and do not wish to have included in the discussion, and remembering that you have already defined your own needs, wants and desires, you have to see the whole thing as accurately as possible from the viewpoint of the other side.

The third objective is to ascertain what it is that your opponent is hoping to obtain from the discussion. Just as you evaluated your own, you should assess your opponent's needs, wants and desires.

Clarifying your own position in each of these respects is rarely easy but the effort spent in trying to set out the three tiers of benefit will serve you well when you are into the thick of the negotiation. If establishing your own position is not simple, doing the same for the other side is considerably more difficult. So why try to do it if the answers you are likely to achieve are not accurate?

Whilst the positions you can define for the opposition will never be mirror images of their own assessments, you will at least have identified what you expect to be the key factors, where you expect the strengths and weaknesses to lie and what points the opponent is likely to want to avoid. Quite possibly you will be wrong. But it is better to be wrong but still have a good sound framework for evaluation than never to have tried anything. As the negotiation progresses, you will obtain more and more information from the opponent – both hard facts and softer indications of their position. These can be slotted into the framework you built at the beginning and will give you benchmarks against which to measure your assessment and progress.

Many times in negotiation there is a need to be flexible and this is another. You should have set out the clearest possible picture of the influences driving your opponent and then adjust them as you progress. If you have done your job thoroughly, and are in a market of which you have some knowledge, you should not be that far away that you have to scrap completely the views you had compiled about the other side's position. All you have to do is make appropriate adjustments to that position.

We will look but briefly at the fourth objective at this point but later go into it in more detail.

The fourth objective in negotiating is to ensure that your own preferred strategy is followed during all the preliminary stages and when you face your opponent across the table.

Inherent in this objective is the assumption that you do have a strategy to which to work, and that is a topic we have yet to cover. Of course, you cannot define a strategy until you have done a large percentage of the necessary preparation. Until you have collected and collated the information available to you, there are simply not enough indicators to enable you to define your preferred strategy. However, once this strategy has been developed, and you know:

○ how you wish to approach the negotiation;
○ the sequence in which you wish to pursue the various points;
○ what you will do if you are diverted from your preferred approach;
○ how you will handle the difficulties which will be raised;
○ the concessions you have to offer;
○ the concessions you will be seeking;
○ who on your team will do what and when;

then you have to maintain enough awareness of these parameters to ensure that you work within them throughout the negotiation.

But where does this leave us on the question of flexibility? We have read that one of the key requirements of a good negotiator is to be flexible in thought and deed. Can this flexibility be maintained whilst working within the strait-jacket of such a strategy? Indeed it can. All of the points listed above leave you room to manoeuvre; all of them give you ample scope to adjust and replan your approach. If they do not, then you have specified them far too rigorously. That is why your approach has been described as 'preferred' rather than 'required'.

As with every other aspect of negotiation, the art here is to have set out your preference and to try to work to it. If you are diverted from the path you wish to take, you will know that the purpose is to return to that path or to one which will lead you to the same or a very similar outcome. The pre-planning of alternative courses of action and the ability to switch to them when under pressure are signs of well trained negotiators who are in command of their environments.

> *It is always good*
> *When a man has two irons in the fire.*
>
> Francis Beaumont and John Fletcher, *The Faithful Friends*.

While we are on the subject of the formulation of a strategy, there is one other point that is worth raising. In setting your strategy, you must be aware that your opponent is doing precisely the same thing and will be intent on pursuing that. The more you can ensure that your strategy and that deployed against you do not clash, the more you will be able to remain in control. But more on such matters later.

Let us move on then to our fifth and final objective in negotiation. It reflects directly upon a theme we have examined earlier.

The fifth objective in negotiating is that you must seek to achieve:

○ *all* of your *needs*;
○ *most* of your *wants*;
○ *some* of your *desires*.

These are the critical parameters within which you have to negotiate. As we have seen in Chapter 3, the realistic and reasonable definition of these parameters forms the whole basis of your negotiating position.

There are, of course, those hawks who would say that the fifth objective (and they would probably say that it is the only *real* objective of a negotiator) should be to achieve *all* of your desires. However, it will be remembered just how we structured the needs, wants and desires in such a way that they truly represented the outer limits of our expectations and a reasonable middle course. The hawks are looking very much for a once-off deal from which they do not expect to seek anything more than a strangulation hold over their opponent. If at the end of the deal, their opponent dies, they feel that to be of little relevance; they have got what *they* wanted.

It has already been established that real commercial negotiation, whether for a single deal or to establish a longer-term relationship, simply is not about strangulation holds. An effective negotiation leaves your opponent *just* enough to still want the deal and to then want to deal with you again. So we will forget the hawks and stick with our more carefully studied and commercially sensible needs, wants and desires.

El Condor

In this western film set in Mexico after the Civil War in the United States, two men are attempting to steal a fortune in gold that is hidden in the vaults of the remote fortress at El Condor. They and their supporting Apache warriors lay siege to the fortress and manage to dispose of its water supply. After some time the very thirsty defending general invites them to talk and one of the men, Jaroo, played by Lee Van Cleef, goes into the fortress.

He believes his position to be one of absolute power with the garrison on the point of surrender. But the general is a very good judge of character (and has, perhaps, read a book or two on negotiation skills). He takes Jaroo to the enormous strongroom and lets him see the gold. Jaroo is utterly overwhelmed; there is more gold than he had even known to exist. The experience throws him completely. After some discussion, he recognises the wisdom that

---

the general is putting over, namely that a wagonload of gold would be far more than he could ever spend, whatever he chose to do, and there would therefore be no point in trying to take it all. In any event, even if he had it all, he couldn't move it so it would be no use to him.

Jaroo accepts the wagonload of gold and a string of good horses with which to pay off the Apaches and leaves the fort. He is elated with his success and brilliance as a negotiator and tells his friend Luke, played by Jim Brown, what he has achieved.

Luke is not impressed. For a very long time he has been lying in jail nurturing the idea of stealing the gold. He is a single-minded individual and it has become a consuming passion for him. He will not accept the wagonload and demands that Jaroo return it and that they fight on for the whole treasury.

I will not tell you the outcome of the story in case you should see the film. Suffice it to say that there are some clear lessons to be learned from this one incident. What might they be?

1. Don't send a negotiator who is ill prepared and can be taken unawares by the opposition.

2. A negotiator who becomes subjective about the outcome of the negotiation is a weak link.

3. Before you send a negotiator into battle, the ground rules should be clearly defined, as well as the scope of the negotiator's authority.

4. Always ensure that you have discussed and agreed – genuinely agreed – your needs, wants and desires.

These are very clear lessons, perfectly illustrated in the film.

But have we missed the point? Was Jaroo right after all? Did he take the right decision?

Rather than be concerned for the characters in the film, we should go back to the start and ask ourselves if they went wrong from the very start. They certainly moved themselves into a position of strength, but did they then know how to use it?

COLLECTING INFORMATION

Those who foresee a danger naturally have a chance of avoiding it.

Aesop, Fable of the martin and the mistletoe.

We have seen that the first, and critical, step in the process of negotiating is to establish precisely what it is you are negotiating. If you are negotiating on behalf of somebody else – in the role of a buyer in a centralised purchasing department, for example – then you must ensure that you do fully understand the ultimate user's requirements and the flexibility within which those requirements can be expressed. If you are negotiating for something which relates closely to your own work, then you must make sure that you have quite dispassionately assessed the requirements and that you have done so using the same critical analysis techniques that you would have employed were you negotiating for somebody else.

So we can assume at this point that you are well informed and have a clear picture of your organisation's true requirements. With that behind you, the question of information becomes your next focus of attention. Let us first examine the types of information you might wish to obtain and then consider how you decide on the effort that might be justified in getting it.

Amongst the most common information that a negotiator needs, apart from that related to the product or service which forms the core objective, may be:

○ *The supply framework.* This is the overall position on the supply side of the business you will be negotiating:

— are you seeking to do business in a stable and well established market or one that is volatile and unpredictable?

— is there a glut on the supply side or is it a seller's market?

— are suppliers' product/service qualities readily defined and comparable across the sector?

— are supply side pricing structures generally understood and appropriate to this case?

— are there any significant economic factors that are affecting or will affect the supply side and which could therefore influence the other party?

— other than general economic factors are there any significant impacts on the supply side that you expect to influence the opposition's behaviour and need for this contract?

○ *The demand position.* Similarly, the overall position on the demand side relating to the business you wish to negotiate should be ascertained. The points given above relating to the supply side can be mapped across directly and reviewed with regard to the demand side.

○ *The other side's position in their markets.* Consider a range of more specific factors such as:

— their recent performance and success both in absolute terms and against the market norms set by their competitors;

— their accustomed position in the quality/service hierarchy in the marketplace and the degree to which this deal reflects different positioning;

— the relationship between their price position on this deal and the price structures and levels that predominate in the market;

— any plans which they may have to increase or decrease their market share, to move to a different quality or price band in the market or to change the market's perception of them.

○ *Recent deals done which are similar.* But you should ensure that you can identify enough data in this respect for it to be meaningful rather than misleading, which might cover:

— deals done within your own organisation with this or an equivalent trading partner – such deals may arise either in your own part of your organisation or elsewhere, but from where you could reasonably expect to obtain reliable information;

— deals done with other organisations which you could contact – this is often assumed by negotiators to be impossible but is readily (and frequently) done in the public sector and between non-competing commercial entities;

— contracts or orders which have been publicised in technical or trade press – this may have been written up to gain publicity for your opponent, because they set new and challenging trends for the sector, or because they were for any reason out of the ordinary;

— deals which your opponent is keen to let you know about – clearly, these have to be treated with caution but may be followed up in order to enable you to draw comparisons or obtain background information.

○ *Comparable factors from parallel marketplaces.* These will enable you to identify where your alternatives might lie if you do not arrive at an appropriate end-point with this deal and wish to seek an alternative arrangement with someone who is not simply a direct competitor. The extent to which you investigate such alternatives will be determined by their nature and the extent to which substitution is reasonable and provides the outcome which you seek.

○ *The legislative and consultative framework within which you operate.* This is of far greater significance in some industries than others; the negotiator must have an understanding of such matters in order to ascertain whether the opponent has considered them adequately and whether requirements being stated by the opponents are in truth essential. The negotiator must also fully appreciate his own organisation's policies where matters are not specifically covered by statute but have been set down as recommendations by recognised bodies. Without entering into too much detail about specific sectors this might include in many sets of circumstances:

— the impact of European Union directives on public procurement, which cover not only public sector activities but those which in some European countries are in the public sector such as electricity, water, health and telecommunications which experience high degrees of governmental control;

— health and safety regulations, which are increasingly having impact on a wide range of sectors and which are often not well known to many people in those sectors; examples might be the position with regard to sick building syndrome, work in front of computer screens and testing of electrical equipment;

— environmental requirements, which may be legislative or advisory, or which may be exercised in a sector as widely accepted preferred standards; examples here could be energy usage criteria and renewable source requirements;

— matters which are expected to become statutory requirements during the duration of the contract under negotiation; an example of this could be the construction design and site safety rules which the UK government had planned to introduce in the summer of 1994 but which were deferred;

— arrangements with trade or staff unions or representative groups where such bodies need to be consulted or where agreements in place already define patterns within which the negotiation must be conducted; an example here might be that the introduction of certain items of mechanical plant into a process has to be agreed with a trade union, which has certain rights over the design of the equipment;

— other particular legal requirements affecting the production, supply, procurement or usage of the items being negotiated.

"... and beware of clause 13.7.3"

That may appear to be a quite horrifying list, enough to deter any negotiator from any but the simplest of projects. And indeed it is. If, that is, everything is looked into with equal attention to detail and regard for accuracy and completeness. In the great majority of cases the negotiator's own knowledge of the circumstances surrounding the proposed deal will result in a number of the sets of information in the list being available or easy to acquire from readily accessible sources. It is then a matter of identifying where there is likely to be value added from investigation of the remaining areas.

Is there a parallel here with our sporting analogy? Yes, indeed there is. If you were expecting to face a team in a critical match where prestige and wealth representative honours depended on your success, you would list up everything that you needed to know about them and how to go about obtaining it. It is likely that you would ensure that you had observers at all of their matches in the run up to your confrontation; you would obtain videos of their games and those played by other teams with which their key players had been playing recently; you would find copies of all good quality published material that might give you an insight into their strengths and weaknesses and you would talk to as many friendly people as you could find whose opinions you valued.

At each point in this pursuit of knowledge, you would cut off from further effort as soon as you perceived that any particular line of enquiry was not yielding benefit. You would thus have done everything you could to obtain relevant and helpful data but at all times have retained an awareness of the value being added by any specific line of enquiry.

The approach in preparing for a negotiation is similar. You have to know all the things that you *might* do and decide which of them are relevant and likely to generate benefit. Against these potential benefits you must offset the direct cost and effort of obtaining the information, the indirect cost in terms of unmeasurable time, and the lost opportunities which might otherwise have been pursued. But there are some notes of caution to be highlighted here. They are that:

○ it is unwise to assume from the outset that a particular line of enquiry will yield nothing unless, that is, you have pursued it in similar circumstances before and found it to be fruitless; rather than make this assumption, try to probe into all areas and then identify the balance of effort and benefit that each line of enquiry will generate;

○ you have to recognise that the commercial world is changing constantly and that information and indicators that you had previously obtained may not still be accurate or relevant; at least check whether such information is still useful;

○ you must remember that it is better to move ahead slowly, collecting and consolidating information as you go, rather than taking a leap into the darkness.

The Missed Opportunity

Mr Brown	Oh, it's you again, Mrs White. Always nice to hear from you of course but I must reiterate my firm's position. We are willing to do a certain amount of design work for nothing and a certain amount more for just a nominal fee but you must realise that my partners and I have a business to run here.
Mrs White	Well, the reason I was ringing ...
Mr Brown	No, let me finish please. If we keep on responding to no-hope enquiries like yours, just to help out old friends, we will soon be on the streets. You have to be realistic. We have done what we can for you but I have to say that we never saw your company as holding out much hope of anything of a decent size which we would want to take on.
Mrs White	But ...
Mr Brown	Look, you and your people just don't think in the right way. You have to be aggressive in the market. You have to recognise what it is that the clients want. You have to really understand the markets you are in and, to be frank, we have come to the conclusion that you haven't got there yet. Sorry, but it has to be said.
Mrs White	I quite understand. Thank you for being so utterly frank in your views. It is clear that you will not wish to work with us on the £42 million sports stadium we have just been awarded ...

STRENGTHS AND WEAKNESSES

For this step, we can put ourselves in the same position as the coach of a sports team. Having obtained as much relevant information as you can about your opponents, you should be able to analyse the strengths and weaknesses both of your own position and of theirs. This is not a complex task, but can be done by writing down all the aspects that you can think of that seem to impact on such an analysis and then shuffling them into the correct place on a grid.

Here, again, a word of caution is needed. It is very easy to identify something that you think of as one of your strengths but which may more truly be a weakness in the circumstances, may be perceived as a weakness by the other side, or which may be neutral in the analysis. Take, for example, the following possible perceived strengths:

We are highly specialised in this field.

may be seen by the other side as:

They have very limited skills and are not flexible.

We are the largest firm in the world.

may be seen by the other side as:

They will not give appropriate attention to this small order.

Our prices are significantly lower.

may be seen by the other side as:

They harp on about price and ignore quality.

How can you address this issue and be sure that the strengths which you have identified really are strengths? And that the weaknesses really are weaknesses? The first thing is to list them anyway, even if the doubters amongst your colleagues suggest that they may present you with challenges that will make you change your mind. If you do not list them at the outset, then you will certainly never identify them subsequently. When you have made your complete list, you might try to see each point in turn from the other party's viewpoint and decide whether you still wish to have them in your list, or whether you wish to move a perceived strength into the weaknesses list or vice versa.

By the end of this process you will have a list that you are content is as robust as you can make it and which represents as accurately as possible your organisation's strengths and weaknesses in respect of this particular negotiation. Yes, remember that you are examining these issues in relation to this particular negotiation and not in generic form for all negotiations. Your lists might look something like this.

Our strengths	*Our weaknesses*
○ Highly skilled workforce	○ We have never done business with them
○ History of delivery on time	○ Their labs have not approved our products
○ Worldwide quality accreditation	○ We do not manufacture in their country
○ Never failed a quality test	○ Nobody knows of our new parent company
○ New sophisticated production facility	○ Our new facility is not properly on line
○ Excellent integration with other products	○ They only use non-compatible products now

The example shows six strengths and six weaknesses. This seems to come out at about the right number in many circumstances but should not be taken as a definition to be adopted in all circumstances. If there are many more than six strengths, you have probably been influenced unduly in identifying them and have repeated some, noted some that really are not there, or gone down into too much detail. There may be exceptional circumstances in which you have a much longer list of strengths, but in reality they will be rare.

Similarly on weaknesses. If you have too many, then you have either been too hard on your organisation or have again stressed details rather than headline issues. Of course, if you really do have a long list of weaknesses and few strengths, and reviewing the lists does not help matters, then you will have to be a very sharp negotiator indeed to bring in this particular deal at a level that will represent a win for your side.

Now you have a realistic view of your organisation's strengths and weaknesses as far as doing this deal is concerned. Note that we have been focusing on the organisation and not on the negotiator or the negotiating team. This is quite deliberate and we will address the issue of negotiators later.

The next step is to execute the same process for the opposing organisation – again, we are not looking yet at the individuals themselves but at their organisation in much the same way as we did for your side.

You should follow exactly the same process, but recognising that each side of the box will have to be divided into two sections, one for topics that you believe you *know* and one for items on which you have gained strong impressions but are willing to back your own judgement that they should be included in the list.

Earlier, we identified that when you were passing through the preparation process you should loop back when you have completed some of the later stages and re-examine your initial assumptions. Here we have a similar set of circumstances. When you have finished itemising your opponent's strengths and weaknesses, go back and review those which you set out for your own organisation. It is quite possible that when you do you will wish to revise your assessment of your own business – to adjust your own platform. We have already identified that setting these strengths and weaknesses is a difficult activity and you should take every opportunity to ensure that you are totally happy with them; a great deal depends on your having them reasonably accurately stated.

THE SEARCH FOR COMMON GROUND

You are now quite well prepared, but not yet *very* well prepared. You have undertaken much of the essential preparation work; you have:

O defined your negotiating parameters in terms of your needs, wants and desires and established your own negotiating platform;

O clarified and reviewed your five principal objectives;

○ collected all of the hard and soft data that you feel will be relevant and made sure that it is checked and reliable;

○ identified clearly your own organisation's strengths and weaknesses relative to this negotiation;

○ similarly, assessed the strengths and weaknesses of your opponent's platform and the position he is likely to take.

The Team Race

'Right, let's get down to business. We've challenged them to the Land's End to John O'Groats run; I think they will agree to that. And the usual arrangement is 10 people to a team with two vehicles as back up – that keeps down the overall cost. Let's assume they will go for that – they must be expecting us to be looking at standard rules. No substitutes or neither of us can identify just how many there really were in a team. And the runner taking over must be running before the previous runner is picked up. Runners can go for as long as they like; it's up to the team captains how they use their people. Overnight stops at pre-determined locations; all on camp sites – no hotels. First team to get one runner to the finish line wins. OK?'

'Well, it's OK by me but I am not sure they will go for all of it. Should we sort out the aspects that we think they will go with and separate those we think they may have trouble on? After all, they are being sponsored by their company and we aren't. They will have more cash behind them and want to use it to gain some advantage – hotels, for instance.'

'Yes, and they know we have three very strong marathon runners who will be able to cover long distances very effectively. They will probably try to limit the distances covered by each runner, or the running time.'

'But all our marathon runners are men. They have those two very strong women. They will probably want to fix the ratio of men to women and the distances each runs.'

'Yes, I suppose you are right. Well, where does that put us? Exactly what do we expect them to agree on? Is it going to be a race at all ...'

You are now ready to enter the fray and do battle – in the nicest way, of course. But on what ground will you be doing battle? There is one crucial aspect that has not yet been considered. This is to assess where you may agree with your opponent from the very beginning, without any negotiation at all, and where you are likely to differ.

We have discussed earlier the concept of everything being negotiable – the scenario set up by the hawks – and dismissed it as distracting and lacking in focus. So let us start by assessing just what will *not* be negotiated. Where do you agree with the other side's position? On which issues are there no differences between you? What can be taken out of contention altogether? In other words, how much can you agree is common ground in order that you can really focus on the issues that require negotiation?

One of the most convenient ways of identifying common ground is not to simply state what you would like to see – like the team organiser in the road race example – but to return to the work you did to define your needs, wants and desires.

In reaching them, you set out a number of important parameters which you felt would need negotiation. But you almost certainly *assumed* specific things about the negotiation, things that you did not believe to be contentious, things that you would not envisage any opponent arguing over, things that are self-evident to you and to which you gave no further thought. Perhaps you were right over each and every one of these points. But it is well worth listing them and ascertaining whether you are likely to be right with all of these unstated assumptions.

Another valuable reason for listing them is that you will then be able to identify the extent to which there is common ground and the relative size of the commonality when set against the size of the differences that exist between you. This in turn will help you to develop a strategy for overcoming these differences. The approach where there are considerable and difficult gaps between parties is generally quite different from that taken when most of the factors are seen in the same light by the protagonists.

Identifying this common ground specifically, rather than simply allowing it to be assumed as part of the needs, wants and desires process – setting the negotiation parameters – is essential to developing a sensible and productive negotiation strategy.

WHAT WILL *THEY* WANT?

There are still some steps to go before taking up the challenge and facing your negotiating opposite numbers. You have worked your way through all of the steps above and have satisfied yourself that there is common ground as a basis for a deal. Presumably, you have also satisfied yourself that the deal is worth having and that there is a strong possibility that your two parties will be able to reach a deal which gives each of you something of what you want. You know very clearly what you want, the parameters within which you will work and the degrees of flexibility which you have available. But do you have any idea of what *they* will want? Of course, you may have had that in mind from the outset. Perhaps it was:

○ they want to sell us something;

○ she wants to rent the apartment;

○ he wants a pay rise;

○ they do not want us to sue them;

○ they want to set up a long-term partnership deal.

All of these assumptions are too simplistic. If you have found it worthwhile going to the lengths of such careful preparation and setting yourself up with parameters for negotiation, a clear and firm platform, and analysis of your and their strengths and weaknesses, is it not likely that the other side has done the same? And does that suggest that their own case is just as complex as yours? With just as many options, elements of flexibility, alternative platforms and, indeed, needs, wants and desires?

Of course, you must assume that the other party has an equally diverse set of objectives as you and that their requirements are complex, with many interlocking factors arising. Your position will be much stronger if you can identify as many of these as possible. The better you can put yourself into the shoes of your opponent, the more likely you are to find the right sort of deal, the deal that will have moved you nearer to your desires and further away from your needs. There is, however, another very important factor which arises in this respect. It has been assumed all the way through this book so far that you are negotiating because you really do want to do a deal; you are not simply wasting your time, having sport or taking the opportunity for some training that you know will not lead to a worthwhile outcome.

Identifying the other party's objectives and wishes from the negotiation can actually help you in reaching a deal. If you want to trade, perhaps you have to open the right doors so that the trade can be done. Perhaps you can discuss things that are important to them – and which may not be so important to you – and resolve them to make them feel that the deal is within reach and worth working for. Clearly, you will not be able to spell out the other party's needs, wants and desires as clearly as you can define your own, but you must try to achieve as near to that position as possible. If this requires some assumptions about their position, then make those assumptions but remember that you did. Test such assumptions as early as you can in the later processes in order to know whether your assessment was appropriate.

Here, a word of caution is necessary. When you have obtained the clearest possible picture of your opponent's position, continue to recognise that it is only guesswork, based on a certain amount of hard data and a lot of supposition. Perhaps you have also used hearsay from others and opinions that you have been unable to check for accuracy. Never let this preparation move you into a position where you are convinced that you *know* the other side's position, starting points and objectives. You will not know that until the negotiation is over and even then you will only know part of it.

This may appear to be a serious and worrying contradiction. On the one hand, spend a lot of time and effort establishing just what approach will be used against you and then treat it as so uncertain that you ignore it. This is not quite the picture. The opposing case should not be ignored – indeed, it provides an important element for your initial strategy – but it must be accepted that your view of your opponent's thinking is a speculative scenario that requires testing and proving. As you progress through the negotiation, you will be able to ascertain whether your start point was appropriate, relevant and useful. You will make changes from that start point to reflect what you have learned and to respond to the way the negotiation seems to be progressing. You will also find that the various lines of thought you have gone through will stand you in good stead later as things develop.

The Formal Presentation

A colleague of mine had to give a presentation to an important client who was looking to place a large order and set up a longer-term relationship. The business had great significance to us as it would secure a valuable base level of income and could be used to show others that we had taken market leadership in such services.

He and his team invited a number of us to a dry run of the presentation that would be made and asked us to try to think like the client. We were to listen to the presentation and then ask questions, which could be as difficult as we liked. Relishing the opportunity, the other members of the invited panel and I set about thinking up the most awkward questions we could – not just to be difficult, but to put the team through the best test we could devise.

When the team returned from the real presentation, they expressed the opinion that the dry run had been a lot tougher than the real thing. Apparently, none of the questions asked by the dummy panel had been raised on the day by the client in precisely the form we had put them, but the team had benefited from handling our difficult questions and trying to see what might be at the back of them.

The preparation had been invaluable in preparing the minds of those presenting and allowing them to begin to think about the project from the real live panel's point of view.

Did they get the job? Of course they did, or this story would not be here!

BARGAINING OPPORTUNITIES

Bis dat qui cito dat.
(He gives twice who gives soon.)

Publilius Syrus, attributed proverb.

There are those who will say that the whole purpose of negotiating is to exchange concessions in order to move separately towards a mutually agreeable goal. There is some truth in that, but it is not always necessary to *exchange* concessions. Often concessions can be obtained without giving anything first or in return. And, of course, much of the purpose of negotiating is to obtain information that can be used then or subsequently for obtaining concessions. There is no argument, however, over the main issues here; granting and gaining concessions is a major factor in negotiating, but no negotiator should permit a state of mind that says that concessions have to be granted for other concessions to be gained.

What you do not know you have, you cannot give away, even when you would have wished to and even when the success of the negotiation depends on it. It is, therefore, an integral step in the planning process to identify the key areas where concessions may be given and where they may be sought.

The well planned and prepared negotiator has most of the ammunition already available at this point. The needs, wants and desires that have been defined will contain within them all of the topics that should arise in the concession process. After all, the two ends of that spectrum demonstrate the extent to which you might be willing to give concessions and the extent to which you think you might be in a position to receive them. It is only necessary to divide up the needs, wants and desires that you have specified earlier into packages that could be taken separately and over which you will have to negotiate. It is on these packages that the exchange of concessions will take place, together with any others that you did not think of but which your opponent wishes to bring into the reckoning.

Identifying concessions that you might be willing to give, and those which you will seek to receive should not be too difficult by this stage of preparation, therefore. The real test of your negotiating skill arises in trying to obtain concessions without giving them and in exchanging a small one for a large one.

The issue of concession-swapping and the techniques and counters to those techniques will be discussed later. Meanwhile, to complete the chapter on preparation for negotiation, it is necessary to look at the question of who should be carrying out the negotiation.

YOUR TEAM

And there's a hand my trusty fiere,
And gie's a hand o' thine.

Robert Burns, *Auld Lang Syne*.

You now have a very clear understanding of what you will be negotiating, the business and competitive environment in which you will be working, your strengths and weaknesses and those of your opposite number or numbers. In particular, you will have a picture of the extent to which the negotiation will be pursued over technical or commercial grounds and the types of issues you will be called upon to handle. In short, you are now in a position to decide whether this should be a game of singles or a team event. As yet, you do not know whether your opponent sees it as singles, doubles or team, but you will have to make some early decisions of your own without this knowledge. You should at least plan what you believe to be the optimum approach and change only if that seems likely not to be correct.

Of course, on a major negotiation, you would rarely tackle it alone anyway for a large number of reasons, so this problem does not arise in quite this simple form. On large and important negotiations, however, there is a parallel problem, namely that, although you will expect to field a team, you still have to decide on how big it should be, how it should be constituted and the roles that the different players will take.

Let us return to the beginning on the issue of teams and address ourselves to a somewhat simpler negotiation than one that will make or break the organisation. It is useful to consider the type of negotiation where it is not totally clear from the outset how many people should be involved and even whether you need more than one.

What are the advantages and disadvantages of individual negotiation when measured against doubles or team play? Table 5.1 sets out some of them and, from it, negotiators will be able to identify some of the principal reasons for having more than one person present in most serious negotiations.

Table 5.1 Individual as against team negotiation

Advantages	*Disadvantages*
○ Need to communicate between colleagues during the negotiation is eliminated.	○ Only one person is available to listen and pick up the opportunities offered.
○ Potential for contradicting each other does not arise.	○ The range of skills available in one person is limited.
○ No confusion of roles and functions on the team.	○ If the negotiator is not available, perhaps for a long time, things have to stop.
○ No conflicts during the negotiation as to how it should be managed.	○ One person finds it difficult to listen, contribute, take notes and evaluate.
○ No possibility of the opponent developing differences between your players.	○ There is nobody for the interviewer to review successes and failures with.

When deciding whether a team is required, and what should be its constitution if one is, it is wise to examine the extent to which your own skills are adequate or largely so for the task. If you are managing negotiators, then you will need to carry through this examination in respect of the prime person you are expecting to send into the negotiation. You will also have to consider whether to change the individual or some of the team members during the negotiation. With a correctly chosen team, it will never be necessary to change *all* team members during a negotiation, so teams do enable you to achieve a degree of continuity. On the other hand, where one person is to negotiate alone, it will usually be preferable to leave that single person to handle things throughout – even if support is provided from time to time from specialists or a note-taker.

Unless a team has had the opportunity to work together, inviting them to undertake a negotiation of significance or any particular degree of difficulty may be hazardous. Train a team on a simpler negotiation, or one where there is not too much at stake, and thereby prepare them for the more complex sessions.

Negotiation is one sport where you have the choice of playing solo or recruiting a team. Your choice will depend on:

○ your own skills – but be realistic about them;

○ the skills of the people you might bring on board;

○ the need to develop others by training on the job;

○ the complexity of the topic and the technical expertise needed;

○ the number that the opponents might bring;

○ the extent to which the negotiation might be long and exhausting;

○ how difficult and tricky your opponents might be;

○ whether your opponents will think you serious without a team;

○ the balance of cost, benefit and risk.

Teamwork

When playing the game of bridge, each side's convention for bidding has to be declared to the other side so that there are no secret signals and hidden messages. Competent players who have been playing together for some time, however, learn the additional signals that their partners will give, such as playing particular sequences of cards when they are in defence. There is nothing against the rules in this but gives the players who are familiar with each other a distinct advantage over less experienced pairs. Many nuances can be introduced into play that will be missed by the opponents, simply because of the understanding that has been developed.

If an experienced player is partnered with someone less knowledgeable, and continues to assume that all of the signals that are sent are being understood, then the play can become untidy, illogical and will probably lead to far fewer tricks than if the experienced player had taken the simpler approach. Even worse, if the experienced player begins to read into his partner's play signals that were not there, and responds accordingly to them, some quite wrong cards can be played, again leading to lost tricks and lost matches.

The 'post-mortem' is quite common in bridge, a pair going back over a hand they have just played and examining why it went wrong. There are interesting parallels here with negotiation.

West	I played the six and then the two; did you see them?
East	Yes, I thought that meant I should take the trick and play back your original lead.
West	No, quite the opposite. It meant I wanted a complete change of suit.
East	Sorry. I was having to guess why you were playing the cards that you were.
West	It would have been better if you had left the room and I had played both hands.
East	Now, look here. There's no need to be offensive. It's ...
West	No. Stop. Don't you dare say that it's only a game ...

Although you may be influenced by the number of people you know or suspect will be fielded by your opponent, your decision on the numbers on your side should depend almost entirely on your own perception of need and advantage. Do not feel that you must always match the other party – it is quite possible that they have made the wrong decision and there is no reason for you to follow them before you know. However, overall, remain flexible. If you have decided to go in to bat alone and you discover soon after that you need another person alongside you, then change, as long as it is not done in a panic and leaves the other person on your side exposed and lacking in briefing – at best unproductive and at worst dangerous to your case.

6

Strategy and tactics

If establishing where you are relative to your own past and predicting your future trajectory is difficult, assessing your position in relation to your competitors' strengths, weaknesses, position and strategies is even more so... Not only do you have to work out where your competitors stand at present, but you also have to try and project their future course in the same way you have projected your own and look at how this will affect your own policies in the future... The greatest help in setting a strategy is a hefty slice of cynicism and the openness of mind to re-examine cherished beliefs.

John Harvey-Jones, *Making it Happen – Reflections on Leadership.*

WHAT IS A STRATEGY?

The word 'strategy' has become much over-used and a great deal of pseudo-science has been drawn around the topic. Here, the concept will be examined in relatively simple terms and applied specifically to negotiation. A strategy has three main elements, which can be remembered as the three *M*s, namely *M*ission, *M*eans and *M*etrics:

○ *Mission* is the targets or objectives that you wish to achieve. These must be defined clearly and the most appropriate approach for doing this has been set out in the previous chapter. It requires, among other things, that there be a statement of the needs, wants and desires that the negotiation seeks to satisfy. The mission does not therefore represent the platform from which you intend to conduct your negotiation, but the outcome you seek from it.

○ *Means* are the methods, tactics and devices you will use to achieve the defined mission. These need to be defined initially in broad terms signifying the principles that you will adopt, the degree and type of preparation and the general approach that will drive your discussions. Means may include elements of the detail as to how you will put these general principles into practice.

O *Metrics* define the ways in which you will measure your achievement against the needs, wants and desires which have been set out in your strategy. Metrics may include both objective and subjective measures of progress and achievement and should be set against the timescales within which those achievements are expected to be attained.

If that sounds rather theoretical, the sections which follow will set out more specifically how each of these Ms is handled in practice in negotiation.

It is worth at this point reflecting on one of the messages in the quotation at the head of the chapter. It relates to your 'competitors' which, in the case of negotiation, refers to your negotiating opponents.

There is much value in developing a well thought out, robust strategy with suitable alternative courses of action, and using this as the driving force throughout a negotiation. But you should also consider the work that the other party has been putting into their strategy and how they might be approaching the issues before them. A well structured strategy on your part which takes no account of how the opposition can be expected to behave may have to be scrapped very early on when it is found not to be working.

Our sporting analogy is highly appropriate here. Imagine we are hearing from the coach of our athletics team that is about to enter three runners in a 3000 metres race. One has a very powerful sprint finish, one is rather steady and completes each lap in much the same time, while the third can go a bit faster on the final lap but is not over-impressive in the final 200 metres. Our coach decides:

O our best chance of an individual gold medal lies with our sprint finisher who is also the runner who is on the best form at present;

O one runner will go out as a pacemaker but setting a relatively slow pace – this will not unduly tire the sprinter and will tend to bunch up the field behind him;

○ after a few laps, the second runner will take over as pacemaker and set somewhat faster times, just to get rid of the weaker runners in the race and avoid the slowish pacemaker being passed by an impatient field;

○ then, towards the end, our sprinter will take to the front, devastate the field and bring home the gold.

Truly a great strategy? Not so. It ignores the fact that one of the other coaches has already decided to send out his own pacemaker to set a cracking pace from the start, mainly to break the field early and leave his own runners more opportunity to use their talent and initiative to take the medal positions. Our strategy is now a shambles. As soon as the starter's gun goes off, we know that everything we have planned is irrelevant. We have no strategy; our runners are out there on their own.

What is the answer? What should our coach have decided? First, he should have examined the opposition, their abilities as runners, their previous performances, their earlier strategies, how they have been implemented and how successful they have been. What would be the right strategy in this case? I have no idea – this is a book about negotiation not athletics, but the message for athletics coaches is the same as for negotiators – your strategy is of no use if you do not also consider what the other party will do. Limiting yourself to your own thoughts is a dangerous fault in negotiating.

> *There are more things in heaven and earth, Horatio,*
> *Than are dreamt of in your philosophy.*
>
> William Shakespeare, *Hamlet.*

This leads on to another point about what we have been describing as your opponents. Where you will be negotiating with a number of separate parties with respect to the same deal, trying to establish the one with whom you should proceed, the same strategy will not be appropriate for negotiating with each of those parties. Consider, for example, that a number of bidders for a major contract have put up proposals which each have good and bad points and the choice will be made only after clarifying uncertainties and identifying which of the bidders gives you all of your wants and moves you nearest to your desires. In this case there would be a need for a strategy for each of the negotiations, adequate to take you to the point at which you could decide between them and then continue the negotiation with only one. Clearly, these strategies should allow for the fact that you will not know at the outset who will be successful and must not yield anything for bidders which might be used during the second – post-selection – stage.

A strategy is, therefore, a statement of your requirements, how you will achieve them and the means of measuring your progress – that is, your mission, means and metrics. It must be customised to a particular negotiation with a particular opponent and take full account of the approaches that might be used against you in that negotiation.

WHY HAVE A STRATEGY?

The emphasis being placed on strategic planning today ... reflects the proposition that there are significant benefits to gain through an explicit *process of formulating strategy, ... directed at some common set of goals.*

Michael E. Porter, *Competitive Strategy.*

If you do not know where you wish to go, there is little chance that you will ever arrive there and, even if you do by accident arrive, you will probably not recognise that you have. While this is true for map-reading and navigation, it is equally true for negotiation. The strategy sets out your objective and the route you expect to follow. It has to be clear not only to you but to those others who will support you throughout the negotiation, whether actually dealing with the other party, advising you or collecting information that you will use. If you expect to have a team involved in the process, including the face-to-face elements, then the strategy can prevent confusion over the ends you have in view, the means that will be used to achieve those ends, the pace at which you expect to move and the extent to which you have achieved intermediate stages and can sensibly move on to other matters.

In business generally, and in negotiation in particular, there are many who believe that they can drive forward simply by knowing about their surroundings and reacting to whatever occurs, taking opportunities where they find them. While that may work for one-person businesses, it begins to fail when others have to become involved in the management or operation of the enterprise. They do require to know what the business is about and where it is expected to go or they will each be taking instant decisions which will point the business in different, and often conflicting, directions.

We have all seen smaller businesses which have been developed on the ability, drive, personality and flair of a single person that have then floundered when they have become too large for all of the ideas to be kept in one head. Some such businesses have survived that expansion, because the person who was the driving force was able to impart the underlying philosophy and objectives to others. Thus, the business did have a strategy, although it is likely that nobody realised it at the time.

The Flying Grey Squirrel

In the northern regions of Russia and Finland lives an animal that is known as the flying grey squirrel. While it is a form of squirrel and is grey, it does not strictly speaking fly.

The animal has large eyes, an acute sense of smell and observers have concluded that it must have some form of echo sounding device that tells it when hard objects are near – rather like a bat. The squirrel comes out after dark and forages for food and the beard moss and other materials from which it makes its home. It has no wings but between its short front and rear legs are webs of skin that can be retracted or extended according to need.

The squirrel travels at high level from tree to tree by launching itself into space and gliding around. It operates in darkness and anyway is short sighted and cannot see a target when it sets off, but has confidence that as it progresses through the air, it will find something to cling on to. All its senses will be brought into play to achieve this. Of course, if it set off from one tree because it could not find what it wanted there, it has no real idea that it will find anything better on the next. It simply launches and hopes.

It does not require a degree in aeronautics to recognise that the squirrel lives with a number of problems. What if there is no other tree nearby? What if it was on the edge of the forest and went outwards? How does it ever find its way back to its own nest? And what if it launches itself from its secure tree and into space just as an aerial predator is overhead looking for its evening meal?

In negotiation, setting off without a strategy may allow you to react and gain ground, particularly if you are working completely alone, but is more likely to leave you at the mercy of a shrewd opponent who sees the opportunity to lead you along paths that you might not have chosen for yourself. Lack of a negotiating strategy leaves you not knowing precisely where you wish to go or how you will go about getting there. You just have to hope that enough goes right to enable you to come to a deal that you can sell to others and justify to yourself.

The negotiator without a strategy is like the flying grey squirrel. Maybe there is something out there that you will find to cling on to, maybe the alertness of the senses will identify something that you want, maybe everything will turn out right. Maybe.

You might argue that the flying squirrel has survived to the present time so there must be something to be said for its approach to life. True. But we do not know how many are spreadeagled out there on the open plains alongside the forests they inhabited or how many have been gobbled up by the predators that are all around them. Negotiation is not about doing just enough to survive; it is about adding to the competitive edge of your organisation and enhancing value in the deals you manage. The flying grey squirrel is unfortunately a dying species.

DEFINING THE MEANS

By different methods different men excel;
But where is he who can do all things well?

Charles Churchill, *Epistle to William Hogarth*.

It is assumed that you have defined clearly your needs, wants and desires and that you have a clear picture of what they suggest in terms of the final deal you hope to do. By this point you should also have developed a clear picture of what the deal could mean to your organisation and its business in the longer term. Are you in fact seeking just a deal or the first steps in a relationship? Does this deal build on a relationship that is already in place? Are you in such a strong position, with most of the cards to play, that you have to ensure that your negotiating counterpart receives a reasonable deal that will be acceptable back at his parent organisation? This, then is the definition of your *mission*.

Having identified that you need a strategy and what the key components of it are, you are ready to build the *means* for achieving that strategy, and developing the platform from which you will negotiate. In relation to the quotation given above, the means are your technique for ensuring that you *can* do all things well or, at least, to the very best of your ability.

There are 12 key points to work through in considering the means. They should all be examined with regard to any negotiation, although some will be more important at any specific stage than others. In addition, you will find that you have to clarify a number of these points in working through the processes that you completed before coming to address the means – so these do not represent 12 new things to take on board.

The relationship between the topics is shown in Figure 6.1, indicating that some can be considered at the same time as others, while elsewhere it is necessary to work progressively through the items one by one. Each of the topics in the illustration will be examined briefly in turn.

1. *Relative importance*. Examine which of the topics that you are likely to be negotiating are the most important to you and which have less relevance. The purpose is to establish in your mind a 'hierarchy of significance' that will influence much of your subsequent thinking and reactions to the other party's negotiating approach. Clearly, the hierarchy that you set up must include any topics which you will not specifically wish to discuss but which the other side may put on the table.

2. *Progressive agreement*. There will be topics which you will wish to have agreed *before* passing on to others. Perhaps these critical topics hold the key to subsequent issues or you may wish to treat them as tests of the other party's sincerity and willingness to compromise. A good example could be where a formal tender from your preferred supplier had omitted a key element. In fairness to others, it cannot be put in after tendering and you wish to know whether the bidder will confirm his bid, even with the omission.

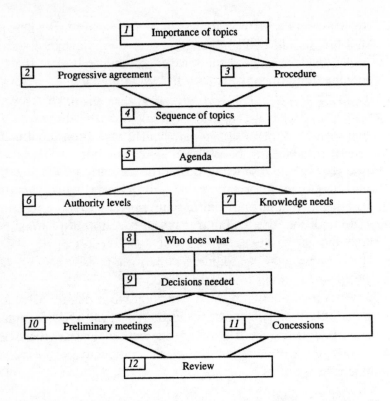

Figure 6.1 Developing a negotiating strategy: the 'means'.

3. *Procedure*. This defines broadly the formality of the discussion and means of achieving agreement. Issues to be covered under this heading could include:

○ the possibility of agreeing an overall agenda and timescale before you start the rounds of intensive negotiation;

○ whether you agree prior to each meeting the items to be covered and subsequently exchange minutes;

○ whether areas of agreement will be considered as cast in stone or remain flexible and subject to change right up to the final point of agreement;

○ how you should pursue preliminary matters, perhaps in writing, by telephone or through exploratory sessions.

Such matters need not be agreed at the outset with the other side but should be clarified from your own viewpoint and the underlying reasons for the selected procedure be known to all members and major contributors to your team.

4. *Sequence of topics.* This requires a plan that sets out the order in which you will raise the different topics to be discussed. This will take account of any topics which have been identified as crucial to achieving progressive agreement but will also recognise that, while discussing certain of the early points, you will wish to obtain information that will be useful when you come to others. In addition, your definition of the running order will reflect the fact that there will be topics in respect of which you may have to give ground and which could weaken your subsequent arguments on other topics. Selection of the sequence should allow you to move progressively through the negotiation, revealing only what you wish of your hand at any time while exposing as much of the opponent's as possible.

On this point in considering the question of sequence, it is worth noting that many negotiators prefer to start with relatively easy points that they expect to be agreed without much give and take from either side. This enables both parties to become more relaxed, to take the pulse of the meeting and to begin to build something positive before they reach the more difficult issues.

It is useful to be able to sketch out the sequence in which you hope to discuss and agree the more significant negotiation topics, both to help you obtain a better picture yourself and to provide a means of communication to other team members and contributors. Networking, an approach which is simple to learn but very powerful in practice for establishing an appropriate sequence, is discussed in Appendix 1, where a case study illustrating the use of the technique is given.

5. *Agenda.* This is the formalisation of the definition of sequence which you have identified. The agenda will be that which you expect to persuade the other side to accept or, if you decide not to issue it, which you intend to develop progressively as the negotiation proceeds. It is usually sufficient – and probably better – to issue only an outline agenda indicating just the broad

topics to be covered as this gives you the opportunity of operating within it in a flexible way. The deliberate omission of agenda items as a device to enable you to throw them in when they are not expected will soon be seen as a trick and can result in your agenda being set aside and the other side's more complete agenda being followed.

Let all things be done decently and in order.

The Bible, I Corinthians.

6. *Authority levels.* This is a point which reflects certain of the issues discussed earlier. The scope and significance of the negotiation will at this point be very clear and the level of authority which will be needed in order that agreements can be reached and commitments made should be assessed. If it is decided positively not to provide the individual or team with appropriate authority, then that should be a strategic decision based on the facts and needs of the situation. The negotiator will then have to plan accordingly and allow for certain decisions to be deferred or for elements of the negotiation to be pursued by others with suitable authority.

7. *Knowledge needs.* A clear picture of the issues to be negotiated and the level of agreement to be sought provides an indication of the knowledge base that will feed the negotiation. This knowledge should include commercial awareness, technical expertise and an understanding of the organisation's business policies and its financial dealings.

8. *Who does what.* The extent to which you will require a team or an individual will be apparent at this stage. The individual might need to refer to others with appropriate expertise, and may need to refer back for approval or authority, but the sole negotiator route might be considered preferable to that of involving extra people in the discussion. Alternatively, it could be clear that more than one person will be necessary in order to handle the technical nature of topics, the commercial complexity, the volume of information to be handled or simply the cut and thrust style that is expected to develop.

9. *Decisions needed.* As the negotiation progresses, decisions as regards acceptable agreements will be required – perhaps on

technical, commercial or policy matters. This is not only a question of authority levels but is a combination of that, the level of knowledge available and the extent to which the inherent flexibility required by the negotiator may begin to change the nature of the agreement from that which had been envisaged. While it will never be possible to predict all of the decisions that will be required during a negotiation, an appreciation of their likely significance, magnitude and scope will enable the negotiator to be armed with the information necessary for taking most of the decisions and to know the method by which others should be addressed elsewhere.

10. *Preliminary meetings.* Following on from the work that was done to define the procedures governing the negotiation, there may be seen to be a need for preliminary meetings – perhaps to ensure that the negotiation really should be taking place, perhaps to identify the main areas of difference, perhaps to sweep away easily some of the factors that would otherwise confuse the picture, or perhaps to ensure that all information that can reasonably be expected at this time is available. Preliminary meetings can also be used to open the probing of the other person's position without giving away your own.

11. *Concessions.* These are considered by some to be all there is to negotiation – the exchange of concessions being the very essence of negotiation. More correctly, the *gaining* of appropriate concessions should be your primary purpose during negotiation, but you should be prepared and knowledgeable about those concessions which you can give away as well. The principal concessions available for you to grant will be identified from your package of needs, wants and desires but they have to be developed so that they are separate and clear, rather than lodged in the overall limits which specify your mission.

12. *Review.* The final stage is to re-examine the whole strategy that has been defined and ensure that it hangs together as an entity and that all the elements are consistent. It is worthwhile at this point also examining how the strategy might stand up in practice. Throughout its development the views of your opponents should have been taken into account and each decision taken should have reflected your ideas of the other side's likely actions and reactions. Prior to moving on, however, it is worthwhile the

team undertaking a final review of its position and of the decisions it has taken.

CHOOSING A STYLE

Style is another element of the means you will adopt to achieve your mission. There are many aspects to style, some of which have been addressed already – aggression and moods, for example – and some that will be addressed later – particularly in Chapter 9 which deals with negotiating techniques and some of the tricks that might be played on you. In this section, it is appropriate to examine three particular aspects since they form an integral part of the strategy that has to be formulated. These three aspects are:

○ leading or following;
○ seeking or giving information;
○ open or closed attitude.

Earlier text has indicated that the proficient negotiator will, among other things, have evolved a clear strategy, decided which issues are to be raised in which order and set out the agenda which is to be followed. In addition to all this, there is a choice to be made between leading the debate or following and responding to it. When considering the various tasks that have to be done in compiling a strategy, it may have been assumed that this would take one inevitably into a leadership role, but the key question here is whether you can dictate the topics and the agenda while taking up a follower role rather than that of a leader. The answer is that you can, if you have thought out how to handle it beforehand. It is no good just hoping that you will be able to lead or follow on the basis of a few thoughts; you have to include the style as part of your strategy and build the strategy around it.

Positive, planned following can be done by encouraging the other side to set out their case and explain their position on the topic that you wish to examine. Questioning and probing, particularly if it is done in an open way which leaves no opportunity to give simple yes and no answers, may then draw out the other party and provide you with further grounds on which to build your arguments. In fact, it may be considered that you *are* leading the discussion at this point, but observers might assess that you were simply asking for clarification of points that your opponents had decided to pursue and that they were setting the agenda. Carefully handled and carried through with patience, this method can be extremely powerful.

The essential feature of this following approach is that you have to decide to use it *before* you start the negotiation. Then you will have prepared yourself suitably and have worked out where you will apply pressure, which points you will investigate, when and to what depth. You also need to have evolved methods of maintaining the debate on your agenda rather than allowing it to be highjacked by the other side.

The alternative of following completely – without a game plan of your own to impose on the other side – places you more at risk as you will not be in control and much of your strategy will be lost from the outset. To work in this way requires a good knowledge of how the other side will react and a strong negotiating position from the outset. The main use of the 'completely following' approach is in preliminary meetings when you are allowing an opponent to set out his case and establish a position or when you are acting as the fact-finder for another negotiator and are not expected to put anything positive into the debate yourself. The negotiator who tries simply to follow the opponent's lead will suffer as badly as would the soccer team manager who sent his side out on the pitch with only the instruction: 'See what they do on the park, lads, and try to find a suitable way of playing against them.'

This leads naturally into considering the balance you might choose between seeking and giving information. Clearly, this must eventually be integrated into your approach as a leader or follower, but it is essential to take the topic separately during the preparation and planning stage. At different times in a negotiation you will wish to give or to receive information. Your strategy should determine in principle when the balance will be towards one rather than the other. Early on it is usually a good plan to seek rather than to give, with the emphasis perhaps changing as the discussion proceeds, but perhaps not if there is no pressure or other need to impart more to the other side. Most of the best negotiators are extremely good listeners.

Oh – I listen a lot and talk less. You can't learn anything when you're talking.

Bing Crosby, BBC interview, 1975.

Somewhat different in principle, but on similar lines, is whether you will exhibit an open or a closed attitude to the negotiation. The two styles come at opposite ends of the behaviour spectrum and can be categorised as in Table 6.1, which shows how the choice of style can also impact upon the leader/follower choice and the approach to exchanging information. Clearly these three factors are linked but they should be considered separately while preparing the strategy in order to permit clear thinking on each topic in turn.

Table 6.1 Alternative negotiating styles

Open style	*Closed style*
○ Offers information freely	○ Offers no information
○ Identifies areas for debate	○ Declines requested information
○ Suggests an agenda	○ Is evasive on the agenda
○ Proposes constructive solutions	○ Lets other side put all proposals
○ Describes the context of the deal	○ Places nothing in any context
○ Helps maintain progress	○ Attacks rather than examines
○ Discusses issues helpfully	○ Demands concessions
○ Appears to want the deal	○ Professes no interest in agreement
○ Considers alternative points	○ Is consistently defensive
○ Looks for concessions	○ Will not examine options
○ Appears unhurried	○ Exhibits impatience

It would be unusual to work totally with an approach drawn solely from the open or closed style. Indeed, an approach drawn entirely from the 'closed' column would be likely to kill a negotiation, while one drawn entirely from the 'open' column might not lead to much success. However, there is clearly a choice of the style towards which you will lean and which is appropriate for any given stage of a negotiation. To some extent, this will depend on the type of deal you are trying to reach, but it will also depend upon the style adopted by the other side.

Overall, however, lies the issue of personal characteristics. You cannot work with a style that is totally at odds with your own personality – any attempt to do so will require too much concentration on this one factor, when the effort should be focused on the opposition's case and the issue being negotiated.

THE METRICS

Under the heading above on 'Defining the means', item 4 examined setting up the sequence in which topics would be negotiated in order that control could be maintained and specific aspects be agreed before others. An approach that can be used for clarifying this sequence is activity networking, which was developed originally for the planning and management of some of the largest military projects – some claim that the American nuclear submarine programme was the first real-life application. In their most sophisticated form, networks can have many thousands of activities, include timescale and resource information and need some of the largest computers for their development and interpretation.

Fortunately, the definition of a negotiating sequence does not require such sophistication and a readily used manual networking approach is generally sufficient. To illustrate the technique, and to assist in subsequent consideration of metrics, a case study drawn from a factual example has been set out in Appendix 1.

The case study in the appendix looks at an organisation with substantial property holdings including a wide variety of buildings, large grounds and the associated infrastructure. The organisation is examining options for using maintenance contractors rather than its in-house labour force. Tenders from prospective contractors have been sought and received covering the next three years' work and the client is about to undertake negotiations to agree the contract terms for this long-term relationship.

There are many topics to be discussed but a small selection has been made for use in this example. The list used here is the same as that taken in Appendix 1 and concerns:

1. a second site nearby;
2. transfer of the present employees;
3. the site manager;
4. resolving disputes;
5. the existing maintenance plant and equipment;
6. redundancies;
7. risks arising during the contract;
8. the duration of the contract.

Appendix 1 illustrates the method of assessing the sequence in which the topics might best be discussed and has generated the network shown in Figure 6.2. This network provides us with two means of measuring our performance as the negotiation proceeds, namely:

○ progress on each activity can be marked on the chart – this gives the opportunity to identify the issues that are next to be addressed and to be prepared for them;

○ reviewing this progress makes it possible to establish whether control is being exerted over the sequence in which the topics are being addressed.

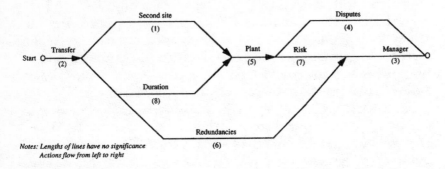

Notes: *Lengths of lines have no significance*
Actions flow from left to right

Figure 6.2 Activity planning sequence network.

In Figure 6.3 the network has been updated to show that certain activities have been addressed and progress towards their conclusion made. For example, activity 2 has been completed, others are under way but activity 4 (resolving disputes) has been brought into the argument by the contractor before the client was ready to consider it. To avoid showing the contractor that this does not fit the plan, the client has allowed a short debate on the question and then succeeded in putting the issue off until later.

This type of updating is of particular value when involved in team negotiations or where negotiators will change, since it provides an easily understood pictorial representation of the progress of the negotiation up to any point and permits discussion on how it should be handled from then on.

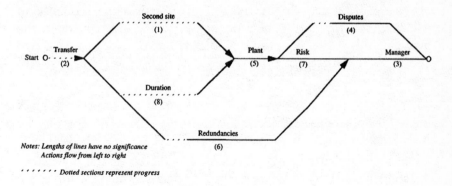

Figure 6.3 Activity progress monitoring.

It has been mentioned that the more complex forms of networking incorporate planning and control features associated with both timescale and resource usage. The simple approach illustrated can also be used for identifying resource and timescale implications, but does not need to be sophisticated or utilise computers.

○ *Timescales.* Where there is a need to complete a negotiation by a deadline, events can be paced by noting on the network the dates by which each of the key elements should be complete. This provides an adequate time metric by which to monitor achievements. In the case study, it was necessary to know:

— by 1 August that the second site (activity 1) could be included as otherwise smaller existing contracts on that site would have to be renegotiated;

— by 15 August that agreement on redundancies (activity 6) had been reached in principle as there was to be a meeting with the trade union on 17 August.

○ *Resources.* If it is likely that others will have to be brought in to assist in the negotiation, or that they will have to complete preparation work as a basis for others to negotiate, the network identifies when these resources might be needed or by when they are expected to have their inputs ready. In addition, the negotiating team itself can form a good idea of their own time inputs and involvements. Again, in the case study:

— the manager on the second site had to prepare a supplementary specification before negotiation of activity 2;

— the client's internal lawyers had to put together their views on how disputes might be resolved before activity 4 was due to start.

Whilst it is not essential to construct an activity network for every negotiation, it is well worth keeping the technique in mind and *thinking* in such terms. This will assist negotiators to assess the best sequence and recognise the interrelationships that occur between the different activities.

A metric which has great significance in negotiating but which is frequently overlooked in training on the subject concerns decision points. One of the main purposes of negotiation is to establish whether there is a compromise that is acceptable to both parties. If it becomes apparent that such a compromise will not be reached, then it is essential to withdraw from the negotiation, rather than pursue it to obtain the best deal possible which you know already is unacceptable. It is very easy for negotiators to become so involved in what they are doing that the results become of less significance than the process.

A primary purpose of defining your side's needs, wants and desires at an early stage, and then refining them progressively, is to prevent any diversion of focus from the required result and on to the process. Thus there will be decision points during the negotiation at which your side will perhaps have to decide to pull out of the process altogether, to choose to talk to other organisations, to make it clear to the opposition that you have truly reached a sticking point or to state frankly that there is a major problem.

In the case study, just such a position arose and had been identified as a key decision point by the client prior to starting any negotiation. The client had certain minimum terms relating to protecting staff from redundancy (activity 6) and, if these were not met, they would pull out and approach the next best bidder. There were other decision points at which the total package of conclusions would be reviewed to ensure that agreements on different topics were not pushing the client side too close to the needs position overall.

This brings us logically to consider metrics in relation to the needs, wants and desires that have been defined during the preparation process. Table 6.2 sets out the client's position with regard to each of the key issues, defining his perceived needs, wants and desires at the start of the debate with the prospective contractor.

Table 6.2 Estate management contracting out – the client's view

Topic	*Client's needs/wants/desires*
Second site	Include/Include and give 4 per cent volume discount/Include at 8 per cent discount
Employee transfer	Direct workers only transfer/All, including supervisors, transfer/As wants
Site manager	Readily available, specified qualifications and experience/Frequently visiting/Permanently working on site
Dispute resolution	Independent formal arbitration on shared cost/Informal independent adjudication/Client's site manager decides
Existing equipment	Select and take at minimum book value/Transfer all at independent valuation/Transfer at perceived value to user
Redundancies	None announced before contract start/None for three months/None within first year
Risks	Agree specific risks for sharing/Negotiate risk shares as they arise/Unforeseen risks all fall to contractor
Contract duration	Not less than three years/Five years with inflation allowance/Five years on quoted costs

Clearly, measurement of performance against each topic will reveal the extent to which the negotiators have been successful in obtaining all of their wants and some of their desires and, indeed, this monitoring is one of the purposes of defining these parameters. There is also a simple technique for evaluating success overall against the targets set. This is illustrated in Figure 6.4.

When a point has been agreed, a tick is inserted in the point within the range between needs and desires which most accurately represents the qualitative measure of that agreement, bearing in mind the target set out as the wants. Where some progress has been made and it is becoming reasonable to assess the likely outcome, a

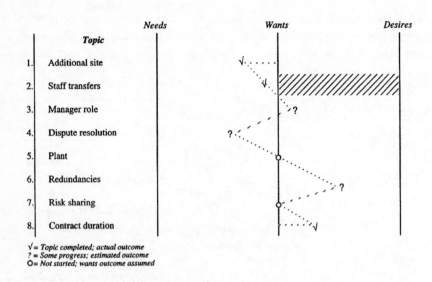

√ = *Topic completed; actual outcome*
? = *Some progress; estimated outcome*
O= *Not started; wants outcome assumed*

Figure 6.4 Monitoring progress against targets.

question mark can be inserted on a similar basis. Finally, where no progress has been made on an item because it has not been started, a zero is drawn on the vertical axis in the centre, representing the wants that are still to be sought. On the other hand, if no progress has been made on an issue that *has* been discussed, there is the choice of entering a question mark in the centre or attempting to appraise honestly where the answer might lie.

In the example, there has been no difference in the definition of wants and desires in respect of staff transfers; the area that has no flexibility may be shaded out to demonstrate that there was no expectation of achieving a result in that zone.

Simply joining up the marks thus made will give a rough idea of the balance of progress and achievement during the negotiation to date. There is no absolute indicator that says whether a good, bad or indifferent result seems to be on the way. Some negotiators have a tendency to place their wants and desires quite close together and so may not show too many strong moves to the right of the wants line; others may give themselves lowish targets but be quite capable of beating them – they will always tend to show achievement towards the right-hand side of the chart.

Another factor that must be borne in mind is that not all of the lines representing negotiating features carry equal weight, so simple averaging may not have much significance. Nevertheless, the chart is a useful method of appreciating, monitoring and reporting progress and it provides a mode of communication between team members.

THE TEAM

Then join in hand brave Americans all,
By uniting we stand, by dividing we fall.

John Dickinson, 'The Liberty Song',
Memoirs of the Historical Society of Pennsylvania.

The question of team against solo negotiating has been addressed in the previous chapter and will not be examined again here. However, once the strategy has been formulated, the team can be selected so that all the requisite skills can be expected to be available at the requisite times. It will be necessary to differentiate between those who will attend the face-to-face sessions, those who will back them up and those who will be providing information from time to time. It is interesting to note that by far the greatest number of negotiations are undertaken by solo negotiators but the largest and most significant negotiations are generally handled by teams of two or more on both sides.

It is not difficult to change a team during a negotiation as long as the people who come into the team are permitted enough time to become familiar with the particular process and can achieve the necessary continuity. Too much change, however, does make it increasingly difficult for team members to communicate, understand what is occurring and make worthwhile contributions. Putting people into a negotiation that is well under way frequently results in them contributing nothing, and can prove to be counterproductive.

In general, if a team cannot be avoided, ensure that it is kept together throughout the negotiation and that all team members are present at every session. Because of the difficulty inherent in this, teams should normally be kept small and comprise only the real core of contributors – which is an excellent arrangement.

USING COMPETITION

Though shalt not covet; but tradition
Approves all forms of competition.

Arthur Hugh Clough, *The Latest Decalogue.*

In looking at the use of competition in negotiating, the range of issues surrounding competitive tendering and post-tender negotiation (PTN) will not be examined, simply the way in which a negotiator might utilise as part of a strategy the fact or belief on the opponent's part that there is competition for the business. Generally, when negotiating after having received competitive tenders, both sides know that the buyer has the opportunity to open negotiations with a number of other bidders and the bidder himself may not know what prices and terms were offered by others. It is, however, quite common for trade groupings or formal associations to collect tender details and publish them to the bidders after they have been submitted and opened.

Even where the bidders do have a reasonable idea of the competing prices and terms, they will often not know of the relative importance to the buyer of the variables in the bids. Where one is significantly cheaper out of a field comprising capable suppliers, however, that supplier is unlikely to be deflected from the principles of his bid by threats of competition. PTN can make use of the other bidders who have not been informed that they are unsuccessful and, the closer the bids were, the more use can be made of it. Some buyers in these circumstances will quite deliberately negotiate with the second or third (or both) bidders simply to maintain a threat to the first.

The use that is to be made of perceived competition, and the extent to which it is to be made apparent to the other side that real competition exists, should be considered during formulation of the strategy. In general, experienced negotiators have found that there are advantages in using competition to help sharpen a bidder's approach but that it is not as powerful a weapon as many with less experience might believe. It is certainly a weapon to be used with caution and, if the other party decides to challenge a buyer to go to the other bidder, there may be more lost in the attempt to use competition than might have been gained.

Loss Leaders

Reluctantly, I include a story from my own experience where I seemed to come out on top! I was discussing with a client some preliminary work that was required before the main project got under way. We were to provide specialist consulting services and had quoted for the preliminary work and the project itself. The client had asked me along to discuss our bid, which we did at length without it being clear what the client was seeking. We then came onto the cost for the preliminary work, at which point he told me that our principal competitor was prepared to do it for nothing. My reply, that I was always delighted to hear of competitors doing work for nothing, was not what the client had expected. Since he carried on the discussion it was clear that we were still in the running. We continued to get nowhere but eventually I offered to discount by around 2 per cent and we did the deal – being paid for both elements of the work. The client's attempt to use competition had been almost entirely ineffective.

Walk Away

While on this theme, another success story. I had travelled to the Middle East to meet a selection panel who followed our presentation with many good and penetrating questions. They then talked price and told me that my price was far too high and that, although they liked our proposal, track record, people and approach, we would have to be very considerably cheaper if we wished to win. The term 'very considerably' put the job below the level of my needs and ceased to be of interest. I told them so, but they continued to discuss our competitors – without really giving anything away. We talked on – about anything but price – while I waited for them to broach the subject again. Eventually, they simply asked for a discount, got a small one and the deal was done. Here again, the focus on competition was ineffective because it was too heavily handled. They might have won a bigger discount had their strategy been different or had the competition ploy been used more effectively.

THE LETTER AS A STRATEGIC TOOL

Many negotiators write letters to elicit information from their counterparts as part of a negotiation. Many others, however, do not realise that the writing of the letter *is* part of the negotiation. You can give away information on your position simply by means of the questions you choose to ask and the way you ask them. Equally, you may give information by *not* asking those questions that were expected. The letter is as important in the negotiating process as meetings and, like any aspect of negotiation, the written word can have both advantages and disadvantages, as listed in Table 6.3.

Clearly, the advantages will apply more strongly if the letter is well thought out and calculated to contribute to the subsequent negotiation, whilst the disadvantages tend to be more acute if such thought has not been brought to bear and the writing is careless and casual.

"Tell them pssitaaa@@**£fffE"

Table 6.3 The letter used in negotiation

Potential advantages	*Potential disadvantages*
○ Wording can be considered by many people and be carefully structured.	○ The other side can seek many contributions to the answer.
○ The enquiry can be put without feeling.	○ The other side can consider the reply equally as carefully as you.
○ The respondent's response can be tested without commitment.	○ There can easily be uncertainty over what was asked for.
○ You cannot readily be asked why you want certain information.	○ Information which is not exactly what you wanted can be tendered in reply, either accidently or deliberately.
○ There is time to consider in detail the content of your letter.	○ A specific request can simply be ignored, leaving you to decide whether to pursue it.
○ You can seek information without being asked for some in exchange.	○ Letters take time to pass back and forth, possibly deliberately.
○ Issues for subsequent discussion can be included to test early responses.	○ There is no opportunity to observe the impact of your words on the other party.
○ Information received by letter can be analysed prior to responding.	○ Substantial amounts of unhelpful data can be provided, with the useful items being hard to find.
○ The other side's reply is in writing and is difficult for them to retract.	

Some years ago the telex began to occupy the ground lying between the formal letter and face-to-face negotiating and, to some extent, to blur the differences between the two. The fax has blurred the position even more. So many organisations now have facsimile machines spread around their offices, and transmission is as fast as a telephone call (but always dependent upon the efficiency of delivery of the received sheets at the other end), that the distinction between writing and meeting is becoming more blurred than ever. However, unless there is a real deadline, received fax messages can be treated in a similar way to letters, with time being taken to consider them effectively prior to responding.

Perhaps there are even new skills developing with regard to negotiations conducted by fax. Certainly there was a perfect illustration given to me by a colleague – let us call her Ashley – who was negotiating with a hotel for the arrangements for a Christmas party. She had been given all the authority she required, up to a certain ceiling cost per person, and within that she had to procure the best combination of services for the party that she could – 'best' being left to her judgement. The whole debate was conducted by fax. Each time Ashley received a fax that she did not like she responded within minutes, thereby appearing to cut off any further debate on the topic; when something arrived that she found acceptable she waited a short time before responding. It seemed to work as the deal on offer improved steadily and eventually came well within her range of wants. Time will tell whether there truly is a new art of negotiating by fax.

THE TELEPHONE AS A STRATEGIC TOOL

In contrast to many writers' and negotiators' views that letters are written *before* the negotiation process gets under way – not a view that is propounded in this book as negotiation has to be construed as including the whole deal-making process – use of the telephone is widely accepted as a means of negotiating.

With regard to the development of the strategy, the position with the telephone is precisely the same as for letters, namely that it should be considered as a tool to be used at appropriate times during a negotiation and with very specific objectives. One of the most serious shortcomings apparent in negotiators who turn to the telephone during a search for a deal is that they do not give adequate consideration to precisely why they are telephoning, what they will say, what they might hear from the other party and how they will respond. They may gain marginally from having taken the initiative but are equally as likely to lose by revealing to the other side that they were concerned particularly with one point and not others or by responding inappropriately to questions put by their opposite numbers.

The message is clear; it is that the telephone can be a very powerful weapon in the negotiation process but its careless and ill considered use can do as much or more harm than good to your case. There are in fact few words of guidance about telephoning that do not apply equally with respect to face-to-face discussions. Some features which do apply specifically to the use of the telephone are:

O If you are telephoned and do not wish to discuss the issue, don't discuss it.

O When you make a call, be quite sure of what you are doing and why and how you will follow up any of the answers that you might hear.

O Similarly, be sure of how you will respond to any questions that might be put to you during the call.

O Do not allow yourself to be drawn off onto topics other than the subject of your call and for which you were not prepared.

O Remember that whatever you say has the same standing in the eyes of the other party as if you had said it across a negotiating table.

O Your call may well catch the other person unawares; be prepared to capitalise on that lack of preparation.

O Decide what to do if you cannot get through to your target; maybe he will not speak to you or maybe he is not there. He will, however, know you called; you should know what message you will leave.

O If you are worried about receiving an uninvited call, try to ensure that someone else will answer and have the opportunity to warn you.

○ Beware of information leakage from your organisation from others who might be called and inadvertently give away relevant information.

○ Decide whether you feel it to be ethical to have your team seek information by making calls to selected people on the other side; consider the possible reaction of your opposite number.

The written word and the telephone can be valuable elements in a strategy but have to be handled as carefully as face-to-face meetings. They can assist both parties in carrying forward a productive and co-operative negotiation or can be used as additional tricks in the portfolio. As with every other tactic and technique, how you use them depends on your personal style and the deal you are doing.

IN CONCLUSION

The key message to be borne in mind when preparing a strategy for a negotiation is that it is unlikely to be right all of the time. As the negotiation progresses, elements of the strategy will have to be reviewed and, where necessary, changed to reflect what has been learned during the earlier stages and what is expected during the later ones. But wholesale and sudden changes to a strategy indicate either a poorly thought out initial strategy or a negotiator who is in panic; they should clearly be avoided.

When it is clear that a strategy is not delivering what was wanted, decide whether that objective is still possible, make modifications as needed and continue to pursue the deal. If it was worth having when you set out, and worth all of the effort which has been put into the preparation, then it is worth trying different strategies until either you find that the deal is not worthwhile or you succeed in reaching your target.

'Tis a lesson you should heed,
Try, try again.
If at first you don't succeed,
Try, try again.

William Edward Hickson, *Try and Try Again.*

7

Managing the process

I want the people to know that they can deal with me openly and honestly. We may disagree over issues, and maybe there's some things we can't reach agreement on. But acting with integrity and professionalism is the be all and end all of negotiations.

Ben Dolan, Head of Finance and Administration,
Liverpool City Council.

There are two principal aspects to be considered in this chapter. They are:

○ those which the negotiator and the team should consider both during their preparation stages and when they are facing the other party;

○ ideas for the manager who is not involved directly but who needs to monitor the progress and the likely outcome.

These will not be separated specifically in the text as some apply to both the negotiator and the manager, while others apply more to one than the other, and this changes as the negotiation progresses.

It should also be borne in mind that everything that applies to your own approach to the negotiation applies equally to your opponent. Thus, when looking at goodwill, concessions, objections and the many techniques available to you, keep in mind that they are all available to the other side as well.

GOODWILL

You and the other party would not be negotiating unless there was mutual goodwill and the view from both sides that a deal was at least a possibility. Perhaps neither party believes that there is a high probability of success, or perhaps there is a greater degree of confidence, but both sides see some value in putting in time and effort to pursue the matter or they would not be negotiating at all. It is this goodwill that must not be lost by any deliberate or inadvertent action, by any trickery or device to gain undue advantage (see Figure 7.1).

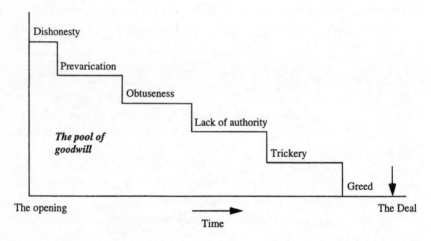

Figure 7.1 Loss of goodwill kills the deal.

While this may appear to be self-evident, it does not always reflect the approach taken by negotiators. At various stages, tricks may be played to gain advantage, statements lacking in truth may be proffered, and quite deliberately misleading indications may be given. When such devices are used, the negotiator must decide whether the other party is one to do business with and whether the deal once done would be in any way reliable. Even seeking a once-off deal with people you do not trust should be treated with caution as it will only be later that the impact of any lack of honesty on the other side will become fully apparent.

In the complete absence of goodwill, there should be no negotiation. Find another party with which to deal – a party that you can trust to deliver their side of the bargain reasonably and whose performance against the agreement you believe you will be able to monitor and manage.

The great majority of techniques used in negotiating *are* honest, even if they might be applied to give advantage which would otherwise not be forthcoming. The use of such techniques should not be seen as undermining the goodwill that is established between the parties, but simply to help the side that used them to edge slightly forward.

Of course, there are dishonest tricks, and some of them will be examined later with indications of how to prevent them doing damage but, where they are used excessively, it is time either to have the trick-playing negotiator removed from the other team or to drop any prospect of a deal with that party.

All of the negotiation management techniques discussed in this chapter would be considered by experienced negotiators as quite acceptable devices to ensure that your side gains from the interchange the most advantage that the other side was prepared to give – they leave the person using them nearer to his desires while pressing the other party towards its needs. But none should be used in a way that undermines the goodwill that is present at the start of a negotiation and which should be built progressively through it.

OBTAINING INFORMATION

There are many ways in which negotiators may obtain information which is expected to be of value in their discussion and in reaching an acceptable deal. They are:

○ by researching published sources and those within and outside your organisation – these have been discussed in the sections on preparation and will not be pursued further here;
○ by asking for information that you require;
○ by demanding specific information as a condition for starting or continuing a negotiation;
○ by gentle and subtle persuasion during the negotiation process.

In training negotiators, it is quite amazing how many look aghast when told that they should be simply asking for information that they require. They cannot believe that they would be provided with it and that the other party would thereby weaken their case. But that is not quite the right way of looking at the matter. If the request that you are putting is seen by the other side as reasonable, even if they do not wish to supply all or any of the information sought, relationships will not be soured and the other party will probably respond by asking for information they in turn require.

Table 7.1 indicates the types of information that it is reasonable to request in a buying and selling relationship but which will not necessarily be provided in the form that it is sought.

Table 7.1 Forthright seeking of information

Of a vendor:

○ What is your whole discount structure covering order levels from small quantities to very large ones?
○ How does your overall order book stand at present and how is it looking over the next few months?
○ What is the significance of this order to your overall order book?
○ By how much would you be able to move on price if we could agree these other aspects at satisfactory levels?
○ May I have the names of other customers whom you supply with these products?

Of a buyer:

○ With how many other vendors are you currently negotiating and who?
○ Under what terms are your present suppliers operating and how are they performing?
○ What sort of terms would you be targeting with regard to the balance between quality, supply quantity and price?
○ Do you or the users have a preference for any particular supplier's products?
○ What else will your company be seeking in the near future that we could provide?
○ What is the deadline by which you have to place this order?

With regard to demanding information as a condition of opening a negotiation, this tends to be the prerogative of the buyer in supplier/purchaser relationships, while in human resource negotiations the advantage lies with the side that gets in first with its request. Typical of the types of demands that are made are:

'Suppliers must submit full audited accounts for the past three years, together with indications of their main financial commitments and lists of their main customers/clients (individual entities and groups) to whom they have provided 8 per cent or more of their annual turnover during that period and the names of the principal contacts in those organisations.'

'I am instructed that, prior to opening discussions regarding the pay and grading issue to which you have alluded, I must obtain from you a specific proposal that you feel to be reasonable and which you table as your basis of agreement. Full economic justification showing the impact of these claims on the business must be submitted at the same time in order that they may be considered before we give you our comments upon them.'

The difference between the request and the demand is the threat, either stated or implied, that no discussion will start without the information that is being demanded first being provided. There are few organisations that truly expect demands to be met but many that know that they are likely to receive more information than if they had not put in the demand.

While requests are reasonably easy to deflect – and you may well wish to provide what is being sought because you deem it in the best interests of your side in pursuing the debate – the demand is less straightforward to handle. There will always be people who will react to demands and seek to provide everything that is sought, but they should not be playing leading roles in negotiating teams anyway. Where a demand is seen as unreasonable but the overall deal is still worth pursuing, the best course of action is to set aside those elements with which you do not wish to accede, either ignoring the shortfall in what has been given or explaining why it has not been provided.

'We have pleasure in submitting the accounting information sought but are not at present able to provide commercially confidential data on financial commitments or customers. Should this relationship develop to a point where your organisation was to be heavily committed to us, we would of course provide appropriate levels of comfort that our business is both sound and well financed.'

> 'Thank you for your letter which we see as "opening discussions" as we had sought. When we meet, we will be delighted to set out our thoughts as to how the company should approach this year's round of negotiations which, you will recall, are each year started at the end of April.'

Demanding information, and continuing to demand it as a precondition of negotiating, is neither a good way to move off on the right foot nor a particularly effective means of obtaining information that the other party did not wish to provide. It is, however, a powerful means of destroying or reducing the element of goodwill that should have been present.

In any event, the competent negotiator will be able to obtain relevant information during the discussion process and, by waiting until the most suitable moment, will move forward without destroying the relationship that has been built. Once a demand has been submitted and not satisfied, either the side that made the demand has to back down – visibly or by creating some sort of smokescreen – or the deal is off. Further, once a demand has been made and resisted, it is likely that the defending side will remain aware of it and be more reluctant to accede to it when it is raised again later. Had the original demand not been made, the topic could have been introduced more gently and more in a spirit of making progress.

> 'We seem to be quite near this deal. My company is placing rather a lot of eggs in one basket with you and it will be necessary for our finance director to satisfy herself in confidence that your funding and other commitments give us adequate security.'

> 'This has been a very useful exchange of views and, although I cannot claim to see where the answer might lie, it does seem worthwhile setting up a small joint working party to look at the overall impact that your thoughts might have on the business.'

The examples serve to illustrate two most useful concepts in information gathering, those of biting and nibbling. 'Biting' describes the attempt to take one great leap forward in gaining information, while 'nibbling' covers the technique of moving forward in a larger number of smaller steps. Either method can serve well in obtaining information but, whereas biting is generally seen for what it is but can nevertheless be successful, subtly executed nibbling may not be noticed at all.

The most important element in information gathering is to identify from time to time what information you need to help you negotiate your case. The detailed requirements will be constantly changing within an overall framework and it is essential to be vigilant as to what can be obtained easily and how you should go about discovering that which will be more difficult to obtain.

Gaining access to information by any honest means is not a device which will undermine goodwill, the potential for partnership or the establishment of long-term relationships. It simply ensures that you are in the best possible position to do the best deal for your own organisation that is available in the circumstances.

NOT NEGOTIATING AT ALL

A popular opening gambit in negotiating is to deny that you are negotiating at all. The idea underlying this approach is that your opponent will then have to make concessions and try to find ways to persuade you to move just a little from your platform. Either that or simply accept the terms that you have stated and do the deal on that basis. Of course, it may not be a gambit at all; it may be that the other side's position really is not negotiable and that you do have to take the offer or leave it. The role of the manager or chief negotiator is to decide firstly whether to attempt a serious negotiation and secondly how to open up the issues that should be discussed.

The most obvious incidence of not negotiating is when we are quoted a price in, say, an antique shop or anywhere else that does not have prices which are clear and immediately comparable. The price is quoted to us as fixed and no indication is given that it could be negotiable. Many people accept that and decide whether to trade or not. Others haggle, but generally from a relatively weak position. In this case, there is no 'correct' price for the item, just a range of opinions depending on provenance, quality, age, appearance, demand and supply, and so forth. You simply have to decide what you are prepared to pay, balance that with your position on other factors such as renovation, delivery charges and so forth, and then haggle.

Is this, then, the only way of approaching an adversary who indicates that there is no room for negotiation? No, it is not. You will have done your preparation and have set out your needs, wants and desires so you will be aware immediately of those factors which do not come within your zone of agreement. You will also have noted the situation prevailing in the market and be able to relate that to the position being adopted by the reluctant opposition. This collection of information will enable you to decide:

○ whether you wish to pursue discussion with this party at all and, if so,

○ the specific areas to be covered and the type of deal you will be seeking.

You should also, of course, ensure that you are fully aware of the alternatives open to you, just in case on this particular occasion your opposite number really is serious about not negotiating.

Perhaps the most straightforward way of continuing in the face of a negative negotiating response is to set out the areas in which you will be seeking movement and subsequent agreement if you are to proceed to a deal, making it quite clear that, unless there *is* a negotiation on these issues, there can be no deal. But, having taken this line, you have to be prepared to walk away and end the matter if there is no adequate feedback from the other side.

In the face of the 'not negotiating' front right at the outset, therefore, you should ask yourself a series of questions:

○ Do I want the deal on exactly the terms offered without negotiation?

○ If not, what will I pursue to try to negotiate?

○ If I would be willing to accept the terms offered now, should I nevertheless try to negotiate something better?

○ Is it going to be possible to have a continuing business relationship with this person in the future?

○ Why is he here at all if he really will not negotiate any of the terms?

In all of this, it is necessary to keep in mind the platform you have built and not destroy it simply because the other person does not seem to want to discuss terms. Never try to prise open the door of the 'non-negotiator' by offering immediate concessions – that *is* a golden rule!

THE PRE-EMPTIVE STRIKE

It is worth looking briefly at this approach now, following directly on from the 'not negotiating', technique because it is another form of 'not negotiating'. In the pre-emptive strike, your opponent appears to have done all of your negotiating for you and presents you with an answer. Because you are offered some of what you might have sought, you are expected to accept it there and then.

> 'Delighted you could see me to discuss this offer of yours because, of course, we do have your equipment installed in some locations already and are in general happy with the quality and service arrangements so there are no difficulties there but you will have to put on the high pressure seals and let us hold spares on consignment in our stores as well as including two service visits a year and the price needs to come down to the discount level you were offering for the larger order quantity even if we decide to buy individual items as we need them throughout the year but then I am sure none of that will present you with any problems so shall we call it a deal and pop out and have a bite of lunch?'

Here again, you have to decide whether the deal on offer is one that you would have been willing to negotiate. Does it fall reasonably within the range of your wants? Is it close enough for you to agree now, save both yourself and your opponent the time that further discussion would take, and generate the goodwill that would arise from achieving a speedy and easily agreed deal? Certainly, a well considered pre-emptive strike will place you somewhere near the lower end of your wants and probably quite near to your needs, so it will be quite challenging.

> 'You have obviously thought this out very carefully and you know the supply position in the market. We can certainly go along with that as we know the way you do business and you have always been fair with us. But I'm not negotiating the lunch – it's on you.'

The more aggressive pre-empt will give you less and the other side more and, if it really does not come within your acceptable range, should be dismissed. But there is a reasonably simple way to dismiss such an approach, which requires you to treat all of the pre-empted points that you do not accept as if they had been questions:

> 'Yes, let's have lunch. But that was all a bit quick for me and I would like to make sure I am on board with what you were saying. Might I take the points one by one? The high pressure seals can be done and I will check the extra price on them. I do not see much problem on the consignment stock question you posed as long as we can invoice you and treat you as a debtor. And the second service visit will be a formality on this equipment so one of our fitters can call in and do a level 4 leakage check without extra charge, but I cannot meet you on the price question. Now, shall we skip lunch and sort out the details on this? Perhaps I could phone my office for the price on those seals?'

If, of course, your opponent does not accept that and insists that the offer is there to be taken or rejected but not negotiated, then you do not strictly speaking have a pre-emptive strike but a 'not negotiating' scenario.

MANAGING NEGOTIATORS

Quite some years ago, I came across the expression:

'Managing negotiators is like herding cats.'

Unfortunately I cannot recall the source but the words have cropped up in a number of training sessions and books since then because they are so close to the truth. Just imagine herding cats. They will not behave like sheep at all. Some will scuttle away and take cover away from the pack; others will turn on the 'shepherd' and the 'sheepdog' and hiss and spit at them, while yet others will simply look disdainful and superior and just not move at all. The final group, just to confuse you, will for a short time do just what you expect of them, but only for a short time. Negotiators will do all of these things because, as was discussed very early on in this book, the characteristics of a good negotiator do not make for good herding material.

So how are you to manage negotiators? First you need to know how to manage people generally, which is the topic around which thousands of books have been written and which will not be pursued here. However, there are some features in people management which apply directly to the management of negotiators but which are not immediately apparent from the standard texts. These include:

○ ensuring that you have the right people involved for each specific negotiation;
○ ascertaining that appropriate preparation has been done;
○ providing access to whatever additional information is required;
○ enquiring as to where the needs, wants and desires have been pitched;
○ seeking a run through of the selected strategy and techniques;
○ checking that there is adequate specialist support available;
○ identifying that adequate counters to possible tricks have been devised;
○ pursuing available options to check the degree of flexibility in the plans;
○ making sure that the negotiator (or team) is not overconfident;
○ playing devil's advocate.

All of these methods can be done using a very positive hands-on style or a more subtle hands-off approach. The style adopted by each manager will depend on the manager, the negotiator or the team and the complexity of the topic to be negotiated, but must always reflect an awareness of the personal characteristics of good negotiators. The approach may also depend on the importance of the topic being negotiated, but nothing is worse than being told constantly that the issue is incredibly important and that a foul-up will have a major adverse effect on the business. If the manager needs to press that line, then he has no confidence in the negotiator and should find someone that he views as more capable of carrying through the task successfully.

We have already seen that negotiators have to be people in whom their superiors have confidence. If that confidence is not present, the negotiator cannot work effectively and with appropriate authority and freedom. Hence the optimum management style is one involving gentle coaching, positive support and light-handed management checks.

The last point in the list above – the devil's advocate – is worth considering further before we leave this topic. If the manager is able to think of the types of difficulty that the negotiator may encounter, pose them and seek satisfactory responses, then the negotiator will be better able to counter them when they arise. Even if somewhat different arguments are put by the opposition during the negotiation proper, or if different tricks are played, the negotiator is better prepared than if no review of likely attacks has been done. This is one of the most useful contributions that the manager can make and any team or individual going into a difficult or significant negotiating session should seek out one or more people they feel can test them fully before they meet the opposition. If the negotiator cannot stand scrutiny from colleagues, there is little chance of success against the other side.

SOLE SOURCE OR SOLE BUYER

During seminars and training sessions the question of sole sources or sole customers is often raised. People enquire how it is possible to negotiate in such circumstances, when there is no choice but to deal with another party who has a monopoly. Just as questions of general management are dealt with in other texts, issues about buying from sole suppliers are adequately covered in books on procurement practice. But those issues which relate directly to the negotiation element will be considered.

There is no single answer to the sole source/sole buyer problem because it will depend on the circumstances at the time, but some guidance can be given from which it will be appropriate to select to suit the prevailing conditions. A key factor to consider is your organisation's position with regard to dealing with that sole supplier or vendor and the strategic risk to which it exposes you. It is assumed that the prospective negotiator has clarified that and concluded that the deal is to be sought.

There are a number of steps that might be followed to strengthen such an apparently weak negotiating hand and the depth and detail pursued on each one will depend on the precise deal you are looking to do and the strength of the other party – the monopolist.

○ Make sure that the position you face truly is a monopoly and that there is no realistic choice for you. Even if going elsewhere could be more costly or less convenient in the short term, it may strengthen your negotiating position and help you change the long-term relationship.

○ Never let the other side know that you are in this difficult position – they may of course know already but you do not have to underline that knowledge for them.

○ Develop and clarify your own needs, wants and desires as if the negotiation was one amongst many for the same products or services. Then, if you cannot reach a reasonable solution, you may have to indicate that the deal cannot be done. Always remember that the other side would not be talking to you if they did not want to do business with you.

○ Check thoroughly the terms and details that are on offer. Do not allow the sole provider aspect to deflect you from the fact that you had wanted something specific and may not be getting it. Treat this no differently than if there were many suppliers.

○ Approach the discussions you will be having as if they were quite normal negotiations. If you do this, you may find that the other side reacts accordingly. You have nothing to lose and much to gain.

○ Always appear strong and confident; always ensure that you are well informed, fully briefed and have a clear picture of your fall-back position.

Finally on this point, it is worth reiterating an earlier piece of advice. Do not be drawn into untruths about your position when faced with this type of discussion. Your opponent probably knows as much about the market as you and almost as much about your position in it. If you attempt to be untruthful you will be exposed and then the deal you will do is likely to be worse than if you had played the whole thing straight. And remember, even with this monopolist, you could well be seeking a longer-term arrangement and that will be more difficult to achieve if you are known from the outset to be untrustworthy.

MAINTAINING YOUR PLATFORM

The final area to be examined in respect of the management of negotiations is the maintenance of the negotiating platform. You have built the platform with research, information collection, development of your objectives and fallback position and consideration of the strategy you will pursue. From then on it is essential to operate on two separate levels during the negotiation.

First, on the tactical front, there is a need to think about the specific topics that are being discussed and how they are developing – whether you are reaching agreement on each point in a satisfactory way, whether you are identifying areas in which you might be able to gain worthwhile concessions, whether you are building progressively on what has been achieved.

Second, and strategically, there has to be a wider view of where the negotiation might be leading: whether your side is remaining in control, whether the outcome currently to be expected places you in your success zone, and whether you have allowed your platform to be eroded or have allowed the other side to move into a position from which they will be able to make worthwhile gains later. If the strategic factors are not running in your favour, then there has to be a review of the approach, of its implementation and, possibly, of the negotiating team members.

The competent manager of negotiations will be able to handle the discussion at the detailed level and to stand aside from the detail to identify where things are leading, how well they are progressing and whether changes in approach and personnel are needed.

8

Keeping it going

'My soul, sit thou a patient looker on;
Judge not the play before the play is done:
Her plot hath many changes; every day
Speaks a new scene; the last act crowns the play.'

Francis Quarles, *Epigram. Respice Finem.*

Everything written so far suggests that there will be no insurmountable problem in setting the negotiation in motion. That is generally so because the two parties have come together to do business and the contact between them gives rise to opportunities to progress towards a deal.

We have examined the actions that might be taken if people do *not* seem to wish to negotiate, or if they attempt to pre-empt a negotiation. We are thus ready to discuss methods by which the parties might ensure that the negotiation progresses towards a mutually acceptable outcome, overcoming all the hurdles that exist, or which might be placed in their own path by the negotiators themselves, either deliberately or inadvertently. The essential feature is that each side moves its position at least a little in order that a deal might be reached. It is at this point appropriate to examine how to create this movement in a positive way to the ultimate benefit of both parties.

CONCESSIONS

'Time hath, my lord, a wallet at his back,
Wherein he puts alms for oblivion,
A great-size'd monster of ingratitudes:
Those scraps are good deeds past; which are devour'd
As fast as they are made, forgot as soon
As done.'

William Shakespeare, *Troilus and Cressida.*

Many authors imply that the art of gaining and awarding concessions is all there is to negotiation. They would have us believe that going to the table and arguing, setting up openings and demanding offers in exchange is what negotiation is all about. Not so. And it is not even so by the time you have done all of your information gathering, established your needs, wants and desires, defined your strategy and selected your team and your tactics. No, not even then. Because when you *are* around the table you have many other things to think about as well as examining concessions in order to reach a deal. You have more information to collect. You have to identify your adversary's needs, wants and desires and you have to review your own approach constantly. So, concessions are but a part of the process and certainly not the whole process.

There are a number of guidelines regarding concessions that are worth setting out because they are in general true – they are not always true, because we have already identified that there are no golden rules. These will be examined first and then some thoughts will be included about how concessions might best be handled in different circumstances.

Swapping

Swapping of concessions is one of the core skills at the heart of negotiating but, as has been indicated above, not *the* core skill. Much of the face-to-face stage of a negotiation is about gaining information to lead to swapping of concessions and preparing the ground for them.

There are basically four ways of approaching the concession swapping issue, and each involves you in seeking concessions from the other side *before* you offer any yourself or even indicate that you have any to offer. The methods are:

○ to define the general areas in which you are looking for movement in the other side's position – for example, price, quality, service, delivery, people;

○ to say specifically where you need a concession but not to quantify it – for example, on the delivery cost of small orders, the rate of bonus payable during periods off sick, or the date on which loan interest payments will start;

○ to give indications of the order of magnitude of the concession that you feel to be necessary – for example, asking for agreement to around 30 to 40 redundancies as part of a pay deal or specifying a particular discount structure;

○ to state precisely what it is that will allow you to agree on that particular issue or the deal as a whole – for example, stating the price target that has to be reached, or requiring specific terms to be deleted completely from a draft contract.

Clearly, the first of these will arise more during the early stages of a negotiation and will be treated as probing by the other side. Their answers need to be listened to with care to identify whether they do seem willing to yield on the aspects you have probed and this requires as much skill at reading the messages behind the words as listening to the words themselves. This type of probing will almost always be countered by similar probing from the other side and it is important that you keep in mind that you asked first. If there is an attempt to divert attention from your enquiry to that being posed in response, you have to be firm and return to the points you have made – politely but positively.

Moving into the more specific area will generally occur later in the discussion but can also arise right at the start. It may, for example, be clear that certain terms in an offer or a request are likely to cause difficulty to one of the parties and these can be focused on without preamble. Indeed, it would be unwise to avoid them or pretend that they had to be subsumed into another area of interest when both parties were fully aware of the major significance of such issues. This more specific probing also arises where an initial general airing of positions has been completed and aspects that could be pursued to advantage have been identified. They can then be pursued in increasing detail.

The principal advantage of suggesting the range within which a solution might lie is that the information is then out in the open and can be discussed. Without figures or specific statements, there is a likelihood that the two negotiators will be thinking along quite different lines.

> 'Sorry. Did you say 30 to 40 redundancies? I had no idea that was what you meant when you were talking about 'restructuring'. I thought that meant moving some people to unfamiliar jobs and perhaps losing a couple of the poorer performers. My people have specified no redundancies as part of my terms of reference. I might persuade them to think of one or two early retirements, but 40 redundancies ...'

The disadvantage of the 'setting the range' approach is that the range you have chosen will be seen by the other side not as a range but as your target. For example, the search for 30 to 40 redundancies will be put to the victims of the policy as 40, but the negotiators will assume that they are arguing you down from 30. Similarly, setting a range such as 'a discount of between 4 and 6 per cent' has little meaning as your opponent will take the extreme in the range that best suits his position. There are, in fact, very few occasions when giving a range will serve any useful purpose, but this is an approach which is used very often by negotiators.

The other aspect of giving an order of magnitude does not require a range to be given but simply one figure as a general indicator.

> 'The extra benefits that you are seeking will push our wage costs through the roof and not enable us to be competitive at all. At that level there have to be huge improvements in flexibility and productivity. I would guess that we could be looking at something like 30 redundancies.'

In this case, the proposer is not defining a clear target but simply indicating the size of the problem that the two sides have to manage and overcome by some means during the ensuing negotiation. There is no suggestion that any figures stated have to be met and there has to be an implication that there are many ways to achieve the desired result. Nobody stands or falls on such an indicator, but the battlefield becomes more clearly defined than it had been.

More specifically, stating the target that you believe it will be necessary to achieve in the negotiation may be a means of clearing up precisely where you stand, or of providing a challenge. If you do state a target as a clear condition for agreement, you must be absolutely firm that it will not change. If you make a statement that professes to be firm but turns out not to be, then you have sunk your credibility for such statements in the future. Of course, when you are reasonably near to achieving your target, it is easier to state it than if you are a long way away. Simply laying out your terms and conditions at the outset is not negotiating at all. But if you prove to be willing to negotiate against something stated earlier as a firm and fixed target, the process of defining the target will be seen as no more than posturing.

Where a factor is set out as a clear and specific target, then you have to be sure that you will not move from it by more than a very small amount. If that is not the case, it is better not to state the target at all but to revert to another approach, perhaps setting out an order of magnitude figure that gives you some latitude for negotiation.

Up your sleeve

'Up your sleeve' is where your concessions should be when you sit down to talk. They should be produced only if there will be something in response, or if there has already been an offer from the other side. Your own concessions should be fully ready up your sleeve because:

○ you have a clear view of your own needs, wants and desires and therefore of the concessions you can offer and of the movement you will be seeking from the other side;

○ your preparation has informed you of the most likely opposing position and where you are most likely to have difficulty in reaching agreement – you know where you need something available to give away in order to open up an area for productive debate;

○ in order to demonstrate that you are in control of the negotiation and have the authority to do a deal, you must know where you can be flexible and where you cannot. Hence you must have checked out the concessions that you are prepared to offer to ensure that they will not be overturned subsequently by others.

Dangling

Dangling is showing the other party what might be available to be swapped if only they were to offer something really worthwhile in exchange. This is dangerous. Once a concession is dangled, it is certain to be taken by the other side somehow or another, and not necessarily in exchange for something you would have wanted in return. As soon as you have shown that you *would* be willing to give away something, consider it as given. You then have to battle to gain something worthwhile in response.

'Look, I might be able to pay another 3 per cent as long as you would accept the penalty clause for failure to deliver to our schedule and guarantee to hold at least one month's stock in all three locations. And that would have to be stock on consignment.'

'OK. Let's put that 3 per cent in the bag then and look at some suitable wording that I could pass in front of our lawyers – but I don't think they will go for penalties. As for that much stock in all three locations, let us come back to that later because I'm not sure that it will really be needed.'

Small for large

Small for large indicates that whatever you offer should actually be small from your own viewpoint but should require the largest possible concession in return. This usually has to be accompanied by an argument which demonstrates that the concession is large from your point of view, and represents a large gain for your opponent. Your concession should then be swapped for a genuinely large concession. This approach cannot be guaranteed to work but does give you the edge as the other side will then have to argue why your view was not correct. In order to know what is likely to be large from their viewpoint, you must have done your preparation and information collecting thoroughly and have the clearest picture possible of where their true needs lie.

Clarification

Clarification of concessions is imperative. During the cut and thrust around the negotiating table it is very easy to believe that you have been offered and have accepted something that was worthwhile and for which you are quite prepared to award in exchange something that is significant. When you come to confirm the position later, you discover that things are not as rosy as you had believed and that you have given away more than you would have wished. It is all too easy to hear what you wanted to and believe that you have just gained something that was never there.

> *'I have a feeling that we are pretty close now. I don't want to sour things for the whole year so I am prepared to make a few concessions to bring this to a conclusion. I will look at separating a flat rate increase from a productivity payment and see what can be done about shifting the holiday pay calculation away from the basic. If you will guarantee continuous working and no walk-out, we'll carry on talking.'*
>
> 'I am delighted to hear that. But might I first make sure I know exactly what you are saying – they are bound to ask and it would look silly if I couldn't answer. Are you agreeing the flat rate increase with the terms we have been discussing; and the productivity payment structure that is set out in this calculation here? And, on the question of changes to the holiday pay calculation ...'

Retractions

Beware of opposition that offers and accepts concessions, appears to reach agreement, but then finds the agreement rejected by someone higher up. It may be a totally honest move, reflecting a mistake made by the opponent, or it may be a deliberate trick to identify what you were prepared to offer and how much movement you had available. There is really only one way to deal with such an approach.

Do not even try to identify whether it was a genuine error or a deliberate one. Simply ask that, as the terms have been negotiated between you in good faith and within an atmosphere of mutual co-operation and willingness to do business, the deal as agreed should be confirmed by the other side. If they will not do it, you cannot negotiate with them again because you no longer trust them. You should certainly not try to agree a new deal because you have disclosed the points on which you are willing to move while the other side is starting from a clean slate, having rubbed off the concessions made previously. In any event, the trust and goodwill between you has been soured, but you may have good reasons to try and conclude the deal nevertheless.

'I am sorry to hear that your director takes that view. It did seem that we were quite close to a deal that satisfied both of us. Clearly we cannot proceed. But I do not want to simply close the book on it. Perhaps you could discuss it again with your director and both come back to see me tomorrow? We either go forward on the terms we had set out, or call it off.'

Total exposure

Total exposure is a very useful trick, but only if you are not entirely honest. Again, beware of having this one played on you. It works like this. You have negotiated for some time for a deal that you both want and feel is within your grasp. The signs from the other side are favourable but they seem to be having difficulty with their own position and perhaps with understanding what the possible outcomes might be after taking account of all of the concessions that have been discussed by both sides. Their senior negotiator suggests that the differences and position options be set out clearly. They start with your position, inviting you to spell out clearly:

○ the position which you believe your side has reached;
○ the options you would consider and changes you might make from your present position;
○ the ways in which you might be willing to help towards achieving a deal.

When that has been run through and is clear, you are expecting the other side to do the same thing with regard to their own position, but it just does not happen. All you achieve is thorough exposure of your own position and your flexibility, much of which is subjected to close questioning, which results in you being drawn progressively further away from the position you had achieved.

If a suggestion is made that you should set out your relative positions and the concessions you are each prepared to offer, *always* start with the position of the other side. Then, if you feel they have been honest with you, you can be honest with them. Never start with your own position and flexibility unless you have every reason to be fully confident that the response will be as open and frank as you have been.

Perhaps the most constructive way to handle a suggestion of 'total exposure' is to take each specific point and examine *both* positions in turn before moving on to the next. If your opponents do this with willingness and openness, you can proceed. If it becomes clear that they were using the device as a trick, you have not been trapped into exposing yourself without any value or return from them. This approach moves you out of the 'total exposure' scenario and back into the more acceptable area of open debate.

The Frontal Assault

Two colleagues and I visited a client in the Middle East for whom we had recently completed the first phase of a major consulting engagement and to whom we had bid for the next three phases. We were to meet a selection panel comprising some people we knew and some we had not met.

We went to a conference room with a large table and were directed to one side of the table. We were still in the process of taking our seats when one of the panel – a man whose capabilities we had come to respect – challenged us that our fee rates were 'ludicrous'. Out of the window went our prepared address, our presentation, our progressive build-up to our case and our argument as to why the rates were totally valid and fully justified. The aggressor continued that there was no point in continuing as we were far too expensive. Then why, we asked ourselves, are we all sitting around this table, two of us having flown thousands of miles at enormous cost and our potential clients having put together this panel to talk to us?

Of course, the answer was that they were quite keen that we continued to work for them and were distressed that our rates had been apparently so high as to make this impossible. We believed that they recognised that the way in which they had sought bids had totally distorted the pricing structures of offshore firms. One of our team had led the previous work and they had decided that he was significantly the best that they could find. Clearly, they were hoping that we could find a route whereby their bid procedure was not compromised, we could charge reasonable sums and they would

---

have the team leader to deliver the level and style of service they wanted.

They were not prepared to say what level of fee concession they were seeking and indicated that there were only small points on the other aspects of the proposal that we needed to discuss, but that such matters could be dealt with quite separately and at lower level.

Eventually a method was found where we could all move towards the deal that both sides clearly wanted, using a mutually acceptable costing model while observing the strict requirements of their competitive tendering processes and balancing price, quality, reliability and all the other aspects they were concerned about.

The frontal assault was effective in that it left us in no doubt whatsoever about the client's principal concern, nor about the strength of that concern above the other issues. We knew that, to win the contract, we had to answer the client very positively on their prime issue.

But there are three other lesson to be learned from this example, namely:

○ We were well prepared and briefed and fully familiar with our proposal and with the work the client was seeking. We were able therefore to discuss the situation productively with the client, even though we were unable to adopt our planned approach.

○ We were initially taken aback by the client's onslaught. We had not even considered that approach and did not know immediately how to respond; our best line when attacked was to keep the conversation going and probe for openings and opportunities to reach an acceptable approach.

○ One of our team decided that we should press ahead and do our presentation. This meant that we were able to pursue and reinforce our selling message and could build in our client's mind the positive features of doing business with us.

OVERCOMING OBJECTIONS

Talks to end the signal workers' dispute are expected to begin within a few days, after a national delegate meeting of the RMT rail union urged its leaders yesterday to shift ground ... to ... seek negotiations 'in parallel' with the union's claim for an up-front payment for past productivity improvements .... Until now, the RMT has insisted that Railtrack address its claim for an interim payment before talks on new working methods could begin. The resolution ... marks a change in mood rather than a substantive concession, but it provides the best basis for talks since negotiations broke down two months ago.

Barrie Clement, The Independent, 19 September 1994.

Not every difficulty during the course of a negotiation should be overcome by offering a concession, even a small one. There are two principal reasons for this, which are that:

O you will end up giving away rather a lot of concessions,

O against some objections, you may not have a relevant concession to give.

If all objections are met by a concession, the people across the table will very soon recognise that concessions are easy to obtain and all that is needed is a string of objections or indications that the matter can be pursued no further. There are, however, many other ways of handling the situation when they seem to be stuck on a specific point and will not take it further.

The first step is quite obvious. Make sure that the objection is valid and genuine, not just a way to squeeze something more out of you. Question it and identify what lies beneath it and whether it is caused by something that can be resolved or something over which you have no control. Enquire about the objection, why it has arisen and in respect of which specific element of your discussion. Invite your opponent to describe the problem and to identify a number of possible solutions which would be acceptable to him. Then, you will together be able to pursue these ideas and seek a solution.

Many objections to aspects of a deal arise through misunderstanding over what precisely was intended. By pursuing the objection and examining it, explaining precisely what was your understanding of the issue in question, there is the possibility that your opponent

'Hello, Mr Simpkins please . . . Ah, yes, I have your letter and thought it worth phoning you. You say that we cannot do a deal because our products contain asbestos. Is that because of the health hazard to your people and your clients? Or are you unhappy about the way it is extracted and processed overseas? Or is it the problem of its ultimate removal? . . . I see, you have a general policy that bars asbestos in products? If you could let me know the reason for that I may be able to set your mind at rest. Clearly, we would not have products that represented hazards or we would never sell them; and our ethical manufacturing approach has been hailed as one of the best in the world. Might I drop in tomorrow and take this up with you? Meanwhile I'll put on hold this letter saying that the deal is off, shall I? Fine.'

will discover that there was, in fact, nothing to object to. Or perhaps you will discover that the objection does not in reality cause you a problem and you can readily change something to overcome it. Or perhaps there actually is a real sticking point upon which you cannot agree.

Generally, examination of the detail of a problem, done as part of a negotiation where both parties genuinely want to reach agreement, will resolve the matter. Once the real sticking point has been identified, one side or the other will see that only small movement is needed to take away the hurdle, or both sides will move towards the centre.

'I very much fear that this deal is falling through on this point. Your contract terms say that you will not despatch until you have payment, whereas we require 30 days credit. It does seem that neither of us can move our respective organisations over this deal because they do not see it as being of great enough significance.'

'It would not be in anyone's interests to see this die on such a small point. Surely there is some sort of bank bond, or a letter of credit, or we could use another form of contract? Why don't we both go and talk to our financial controllers and see if we can't come up with something?'

'Fine. Shall we meet back here at the same time on Wednesday and compare notes and ideas? Great, look forward to seeing you then.'

There will, of course, be times when you cannot overcome an objection as easily as that. If in those circumstances you still wish to pursue the deal and reach agreement, then the contentious issue can be 'back-burnered', that is, it can be removed from the furnace of the negotiation and placed somewhere else to simmer away quietly until you are ready for it. Unlike cookery, when you have to get back to the item on the back burner before it spoils, the negotiation back burner can result in both parties realising that there is no need for a confrontation on that issue and can agree something to resolve it, thereby never really dealing with that issue as it stood. If this is not possible, then nothing has been lost and the issue can be brought forward at a suitable time and be debated and resolved.

While many objections arise through misunderstandings, many others occur through information overload, when one or other of the sides has received so much information and debated it in such detail as to have become confused. Objections raised under these circumstances are difficult to resolve because the objector is unclear about the objection, which is more a defence mechanism than necessarily a genuine problem. Where there is a suspicion that this is the reason for an objection, the favoured approach is to break off and allow both sides to take stock, clear their minds, and reorganise their thoughts prior to meeting again.

There are many ways in which a break can be called for without dislodging the negotiation, in a way that is mutually acceptable and so as to retain the goodwill that has been built up. It is even possible to be quite open about the reason and agree between you how to handle the matter. The wrong way to do it is to try some form of trick, for example an arranged interruption, since there is no need for such deception and your adversary will be dubious as to your reasons.

Assuming that there has been a substantial element of goodwill in the negotiation, a significant objection when you are well down the track can often be overcome by reviewing the points that have already been agreed. In theory, this has no effect whatsoever upon the latest problem, but it can in practice have a significant impact by demonstrating how far you have come and how great are the points of agreement compared with the difficulty that has just been raised. It comes rather into the category of 'Don't let us waste all this effort that we have so far put in.' There is no dishonesty in trying to overcome an objection by pointing out the positive nature of the agreement achieved so far – it is merely an attempt to put the issue into perspective and balance. If it remains a heavy issue which is not outweighed by all of the others, then you have to deal with it as such, but if not, it is worthwhile trying to remove it by demonstrating that its significance is not as great as might have been believed.

A word of caution, however, on the issue of 'not wasting all this time'. This approach also features as a negotiating trick. Consider, for example, the position when your opposite numbers deliberately leave to the end the most difficult point, perhaps an extra charge that you might well have been assuming was included in something else that has been discussed. When you react against it and they refuse to move – generally blaming head office for this intractability – the waste of time card is played. Knowing about this trick is half the battle in defeating it, deciding to throw it out is the other half.

'OK, let's wrap this up then. Except that we have not discussed the spare parts. They are provided at the list prices supplied with the catalogue. Just say what you want when you place your order for the machines.'

'But the contract says that every machine comes with a full kit of spares. That is what I was negotiating. If you are saying they are extra, I am completely outside my budget and we should certainly be looking elsewhere.'

'It's not a mistake any of my other customers have ever made. It is our standard approach, especially for such a tightly structured deal. But this talk of other suppliers will not help anyone. Just think of all the time and effort we have both invested in this deal. Don't let's waste all of that.'

'Yes, it would be disappointing to falter over this one point. But I am in business to get these contracts right, not to make life easy for myself. If you want to talk to your sales director, fine. If the deal is on with the spares included, fine. If not, then we both have to write off the time we have spent. Goodbye . . .'

When you have become convinced that the others truly do have a problem with one of the issues being discussed, and have raised a valid objection that could place the deal in jeopardy, then you may have no choice but to offer a concession. On this type of occasion it will probably have to be a concession for which you will not obtain one in response. Prior to giving it, therefore, you must be completely sure that there is no other way around the objection.

If your opponent discovers that you will grant concessions at each and every apparent blockage, then the number of blockages will increase. The more the concessions, the more the blockages will arise.

Whereas you may receive nothing material in return for clearing a genuine blockage, you should ensure that the gesture you are making is understood and appreciated as this can add to the pool of goodwill that exists between you. You may well have to call upon that pool later if there is an issue on which you in turn have difficulty.

Finally, if both of you meet an objection or hurdle that neither seems to be able to overcome – perhaps there is no way over, through or around it – then it might be appropriate to let somebody else have a go at clearing it away. Such apparently intractable problems may arise for a number of reasons, including:

○ too much immersion in detail by one or other party, or by both;
○ clashes of personality;
○ lack of authority in general or on a specific matter;
○ failure to understand the true meaning or effect of an issue;
○ apparently immovable parameters defined by others;
○ too much rigidity in the position taken by at least one side;
○ a belief that the other party will back down if pushed hard enough.

It is clear that the person to whom a negotiator hands the problem may come from anywhere in the hierarchy; it does not have to be somebody holding greater seniority or a higher level of authority to commit the organisation. For example, when the issue holding up the successful pursuit of a negotiation is specifically technical, then the best people to bring in may themselves be technical, and where they are commercial or contractual, people with those skills may be appropriate. But here it is important to remember all that was set out earlier about teamworking. Simply bringing someone into the team for a single event can be dangerous unless they fully appreciate their role and its limitations. Too many people, once involved, are likely to feel that there are many other aspects that they would be ideal to handle.

'That does seem to have cleared up that problem, then. I am pleased to have been able to help so that our two companies can continue to do such good business together. By the way, while I am here with both of you, could I mention that I noticed this item about tolerances – we really don't need to go as tight as 4 microns and the sample sizes could be smaller without giving us problems, and not only that, Geoff, but I see that you are asking them for a 12 per cent discount on standard types but you know we usually buy at list price less 3 per cent and these delivery times . . .'

It is both the selection of the person to involve and their briefing which governs the success of this practice for the removal of objections. Both should lie in the hands of the negotiator and be controllable.

TOTAL DEADLOCK

However much a negotiator knows about the skills and techniques of negotiation, there will be times when it just is not possible to reach agreement with the other party, even when agreement is essential. Such cases might arise in a wide range of circumstances, including:

○ when two parties have won a contract where they submitted a joint venture bid without finalising all the details – breakdown may arise in trying to agree which services will be provided by each of the partners and how much they will take out of the contract income for those services;

○ after a contract has been signed between a supplier and a purchaser and there has been agreement that certain of the terms will be agreed subsequently, but within the overall contract framework;

○ if a deal has been struck and the work involved is in progress and there are changes or additions which have to be incorporated into the contract;

○ on the breakdown of a deal after it has been finalised and commenced but the parties agree to cancel it, or are forced to do so, and the services provided and cancellation charges have to be evaluated for payment;

○ after broadly satisfactory completion of a contract when one of the parties has a claim for additional payments which the other does not accept to a significant degree.

It will be clear that, in some of these circumstances, the goodwill present at the early negotiations or contract stage will still be present but in others it will have dissipated. In any event, goodwill alone may not be sufficient to carry the two parties to a deal. When conditions prevail that prevent a deal being achieved no matter what the negotiators do, there are still methods that can be adopted to achieve solutions acceptable to both parties.

In the section above, the proposal was put that a deadlocked negotiator might pass the problem over to somebody having a fresh view, greater authority, a wider perspective or a combination of these. Where this does not succeed and the issue is of major significance to the organisations concerned, there may be a case for bringing in the chief executives of the disputing divisions or top-level organisations. Clearly, this should not be done lightly or increasing numbers of negotiations will become deadlocked and be escalated, thereby undermining any standing each negotiator had in the eyes of the other.

Escalation should not require the chief executives to debate and reach agreement on the details of the case. A small range of very key issues which control the overall outcome should be isolated in order that the senior people can focus on them and provide frameworks within which the negotiators may then reach agreement on all of the outstanding points. If the chiefs did try to resolve all of the issues they would become bogged down in too much detail and would in any event not understand enough of the background.

> 'Thank you for coming in today. I hope we can help this matter to move forward. I see that we both have the same briefing papers, so each of us knows the current views of both sides' negotiators. It has been suggested that we concern ourselves at this time only with the principles on which the extra work is to be priced and, if you agree, we will work our way through the key headings that our people have listed here . . . excellent . . . shall we start by looking at when the schedule of rates might apply?'

But what if the two chiefs cannot agree either on the principles or on how the key issues might be handled? Consider, for example, a post-contract claim where one party postulates that it was caused extra cost because of the failings of the other, but the claim is rejected totally.

> 'Your argument that your people could not get on site to carry out the placing and fixing operations is a load of rubbish. Oh yes, of course I've seen all of those absurd letters of complaint by your site supervisor but I've also seen our replies and our site diary that shows that most of the time you only had one or two people there anyway and they couldn't have done the job even if they could have got on the site and I don't think much of this argument that you didn't send more because those who were there couldn't work so you'll get not a penny out of us for this and I am counter-claiming from you for the delays you caused us and I'll see you in court.'

There is a key role here for an experienced negotiator who has been trained to help resolve such disputes and who is independent of both parties. Such a negotiator – a mediator – has the task of identifying issues on which each party might be willing to move, probing separately with each to see if there is a prospect of a solution, and progressing whatever concessions might be available until the parties can finally achieve a settlement. This cannot always be successful, but an increasing number of deadlocked disputes is being settled in this way. If the parties agree to subject themselves to mediation, they do not have to agree that the mediator's solution will be legally binding as the purpose is to encourage the parties themselves to achieve agreement and then mutually agree to make it binding. The mediator does not act as judge or arbitrator and impose a solution.

In theory, a mediator can add nothing to a negotiation since both parties should be attempting to identify a mutually agreeable outcome. In practice, many negotiations, particularly on issues such as those set out above, do collapse and need outside assistance. If the parties will not accept mediation, they may well end up in arbitration or litigation.

The body which provides many of the mediators who operate on commercial disputes in the United Kingdom is the Centre for

Dispute Resolution (CEDR), about which some notes have been included as Appendix 2.

SELLING THE DEAL

It is all very well maintaining progress, and the concomitant good-will, throughout the negotiation until you have reached a mutually satisfactory agreement, but the value of the effort disappears if either of you is then unable to persuade your own people that the deal you have done is within the range of acceptability.

The probability of failing to sell the deal back home will diminish if the negotiator has managed the affair correctly, ensuring that the needs, wants and desires have been agreed with those upon whom the deal will impact and ascertaining where within the range of wants they would feel a good job had been done. Unfortunately, however, attitudes vary as negotiations progress and it is not always possible to read other people's thoughts and how their expectations might have changed. Alternatively, as your expectations of what can be achieved change as the negotiation progresses, the expectations of others involved or having an interest may still be where yours were at the start.

> 'Hang on a minute. What do you mean you've done a deal? They offered us a 4 per cent flat increase at the start and you said that we would not go yet another year without sorting out the bonus, productivity and training disputes. You said that all along. And every speech you made told us to hold firm, not back down, be strong and show what we are made of. You'd better get your coat on again and get down there and tell them you made a mistake.'

> 'I don't want to know all this stuff about needs, wants and desires. You said that we were going to become one of their preferred suppliers with a good steady flow of guaranteed work. That was three months ago and you have said nothing to any of us since then. Now you come back and tell us that you have been wonderfully successful in breaking their monopoly supplier's hold and have an order that will take about two days to complete. Do you really feel that you are suited to this company?'

The negotiator needs to have reasons why every deal that has been done is appropriate to the circumstances. Even a good deal may be seen by others as not quite good enough – it is a fact of life that, whatever you have negotiated, some of those who were not involved will always be certain that they could have done it better. One approach to achieving this 'selling' of the deal is to demonstrate why nothing better could have been obtained but it is usually better to accentuate the good elements of the deal and even to make those that are not quite so good look rather better – adopting some of the skills of salesmanship.

'Slow down a bit, nobody is going to renege on the deal we've made. I'm sticking to what has been agreed or we will not be trusted again. Just take a look at what has been achieved. We didn't say what we were looking for at the start but we have 6 per cent – that's 50 per cent more than was offered. And it applies to all the rates, not just those that are consolidated. And we have agreement to this joint working party to look at the other issues. And it has a deadline on it – they didn't much like agreeing to that, I can tell you – so it has to generate something really useful. If that isn't standing firm, and if they don't know now what we are made of, I don't know what is. Any more questions or shall we start celebrating?'

And maybe the salesperson who had managed to break into the monopoly position had actually achieved a great deal, but had failed to make others aware of what was being sought.

By far the best approach to selling the deal is to have managed expectations throughout the process by ensuring that the likely outcomes were anticipated and any shortfalls from earlier expectations explained thoroughly. If that is done effectively, the negotiator can proceed confident in the knowledge that support is available from the organisation and that the deal that is being sought will meet its needs and aspirations.

PACING YOURSELVES

Part of the strategy that you evolved will have been to assess the sequence in which you wished to approach the issues to be discussed. Another part will have been to identify how long you should spend on each issue in order to grant it appropriate significance, but not too much. In addition, you will be aware that, should any particular issue become bogged down for any reason, it needs to be cleared away in one of the ways mentioned. So your strategy will have given you a good idea of the timescale for the negotiation – indeed most negotiations have a timescale imposed upon them – which has to be taken into account in developing the strategy.

It has already been noted that you should ensure that you stay in control of the agenda, but you must also stay in control of the timescales. If progress is ahead of your allowed target and you have no reason to believe that you have missed something, then you can set aside the issue and concentrate for the moment upon the terms you are discussing. If progress falls behind, however, it may be that there is a clear reason or that a combination of reasons prevails. The causes which you should examine include that:

○ your original timing scheme was incorrect;
○ things are more complicated than you had expected;
○ there is confusion over some of the issues that is not being clarified quickly;
○ there is not enough knowledge around the table;
○ one or other of you is being more pedantic than is needed;
○ one side is deliberately holding things up;
○ there is insufficient authority to do the deal.

The negotiator's task is to examine these possibilities, and any others that might be relevant in the specific circumstances, and identify which are the controlling influences. They can then be dealt with and a new timetable be developed to act as the means of control. Having decided to stay in control of the agenda, it is essential to then stay in control of the pace of the negotiation and ensure that it runs according to a reasonable plan.

As there is a deadline or target date involved in most negotiations for one side or the other, it is also important to be able to pace the negotiation so that undue pressure will not be put upon you as the deadline approaches. On many occasions such a deadline will be quite reasonable and necessary – rather than having been manufactured by one of the negotiators to put pressure on the other side. It is up to the negotiator with the time pressure to reveal as much as is considered desirable and not so much as to put himself at a disadvantage. Often, in fact, deadlines are used as an attempt to gain advantage by the person who raises the question, when the other party may have known nothing of it.

> 'Ah, that is a little difficult, madam. We have received a price increase notification from Ford that applied from midnight last night . . . but our sales director has been away for a few days and has to sign off all orders. If you could place your order and pay your deposit before he's back tomorrow morning, I could backdate it and you get the old price.'

> 'At the end of next week I move to metal purchasing and one of my colleagues will be taking over here. If we are not able to complete this contract before I go, he will probably want to start in his own way – and he is very keen to make a big impression. But if we could have it all wrapped up by next Wednesday . . .'

These examples are illustrations of the use of deadlines where they are intended to give advantage to the side that revealed them. It may also be worthwhile giving such information without an intention to gain significantly and put pressure on the other side.

> 'My managing director has not been impressed with what he has heard about partnering. I want to use this deal to show just how worthwhile it can be for us. He has given me until Thursday to come up with a deal that proves the idea. If you are really interested, I'm prepared to work all hours until then to try to put something together. But don't let's start unless you think we can do it.'

> 'I think everyone here wants to finish putting this together but recognises that we still have a lot to sort out. I propose that we give ourselves some targets for agreeing different sections of the contract. If we cannot meet those, then we have to begin to question whether the deal really is on. Now, by Wednesday lunchtime . . .'

Remaining in control by managing the pace and anticipating actions needed to stay inside deadlines is not difficult if it is incorporated within the overall strategy. It becomes difficult only if control is not exercised from the outset and the other side is permitted to dictate timescales.

BREAKS AND INTERRUPTIONS

The use of breaks in the flow of a negotiation has been examined already, particularly in the context of taking stock and not becoming overtired and therefore unable to assess proposals being put forward. Breaks may also be used to gain strategic advantage, either by destroying the flow from the other side or by ensuring that as much information as possible is gleaned about the opponent's case immediately prior to the break, giving your own side the chance to review it, redefine the strategy and consider in more detail the precise line to be followed.

Breaks may be called quite openly by one side or the other, but many negotiators pride themselves on having many tricks available to create them. Such tricks are, however, usually quite obvious to the other side and contribute to destroying the goodwill that had prevailed. The most common methods used include:

○ telephone calls – anybody who wishes to avoid calls during certain periods can do so, but the expanding use of mobile telephones is an increasing cause of interruptions, whether planned or accidental;

○ messages being brought into the room, which often serve as an excuse to then leave the room – again, such interruptions can be avoided;

○ toilet or 'comfort' breaks, which are needed but not necessarily when or as frequently as they are proposed;

○ unscheduled meal breaks, which could generally have been foreseen and agreement reached earlier as to how they would be handled.

There are, however, many other distractions that can be used, mainly depending upon the local circumstances. The negotiator has to decide whether to simply ignore them – being aware that they are probably deliberate gives the edge in not allowing them to cause genuine distraction from the objective – or to try to eliminate them. One of the most effective ways to remove the worst breaks and interruptions

"The negotiations must be going badly. Norris is trying the old King Kong trick"

is to raise them as an issue and suggest that they be dealt with immediately in order that things may proceed unhindered. If that is not acceptable to the other side, the suggestion can be put that the meeting should be deferred until it can be managed properly, or moved to another place where the interruptions need not happen.

195

The Day the Earth Moved

One of my colleagues was in Mexico City to negotiate a major sale to a bank. They were on the executive floor of the bank's headquarters, high up in their impressive tower, and were closely involved in discussing the detail of the deal. Some of the team on the client side seemed not to be too happy – perhaps they had not done their preparation adequately – and seemed uncertain between themselves whether they should accept certain of the arrangements being proposed.

Suddenly, one interrupted the debate, jumped to his feet: 'My God, did you feel that? It's an earthquake. Get down the stairs straight away. Do not use the lifts.'

Everyone dropped everything and went for the stairs. They had gone down a few flights when they realised that there was nobody else from this substantial headquarters on the stairs – nobody else seemed to be evacuating the building. They paused, emerged at the floor level they were on and discovered that everybody was working normally. Nobody had felt the earth tremor. And what was more, the only person who seemed to have done so was not with them – he had disappeared off somewhere else, presumably to get himself briefed for the next round of discussions or to check some facts.

The party returned to their room and continued. Unfortunately the story does not include any information as to how effective this piece of trickery was, but we can guess.

The question of playing home or away is of importance here. Many negotiators prefer to play at home because it gives them the option to have or to avoid enforced breaks and interruptions and to select their timing. When dealing with people who try to use interruptions as a means of gaining advantage, restrict yourself to negotiating on your own territory and ensuring that there are adequate instructions for sessions not to be interrupted.

One final point on the question of enforced breaks in meetings. When faced with opponents who habitually involve themselves in devious ways of breaking up a flow of negotiation, it is worth asking whether that is the type of organisation, or the type of people, it is wise to do business with. If those are the tricks that are tried when the interest in doing the deal is highest, what might occur once the deal has been signed and you are expecting the other side to deliver their side of the bargain?

At the more detailed level, the matter of interrupting people during the flow of debate must be considered.

○ Should a negotiator be interrupted if he wishes to put his case before you have set out your position?

○ Is it wise to interrupt someone who is in full flow when they have said one or more things with which you do not agree?

○ Should somebody who seems to be taking too much for granted be interrupted politely so that the various points may be clarified in turn?

The 'interrupters' argue that, once the other side has set out its case, they have to back down if there are details that you do not like. They are less likely to back down having stated their position than if it had not been stated and a clear position been taken. This assumes that your opponents will have defined clearly their platform and that they will then be totally committed to defending it to the death. In addition, they argue, interrupting will throw the others off track and give you an advantage. 'Interrupters' prefer to set out their own platform and invite the others to move towards it.

The 'non-interrupters', on the other hand, argue that it is always better to know the other side's position than not to know. If the opposing viewpoint has been laid out before you, you can identify where the differences might lie, assess which ones are worth pursuing and in which order. In that event, you have not exposed your own platform to the other side and may never need to do so on some issues. As to the matter of throwing the other side off course and confusing them, if you can gain ground as easily as that, you did not have much of a negotiation on your hands anyway and could have coasted through to achieve your objectives with ease. The choice remains yours.

There was an old owl liv'd in an oak
The more he heard, the less he spoke;
The less he spoke, the more he heard
O, if men were all like that wise bird!

Punch, 1875.

On the whole, experienced negotiators – who are often different from experienced writers about negotiation – prefer the latter course. If someone is telling you something, then you should be willing to listen. One of the objectives in negotiation is to receive information and, if the other side wishes to give it, then you should be willing to receive. In any event, very few negotiators who do wish to set out their case at the outset will explain it in such definitive terms that they cannot then show flexibility and movement around the terms they have described. When you interrupt a flow of incoming information, it can only be to give information to the other side – even if it is only to question a point that has just been made. They then know that the issue is of importance to you.

> 'We propose to subcontract the design work for completion by Thursday and to buy in the main materials partly fabricated with an on-cost to you of 14 per cent and the quality guarantee would lie with our suppliers but you could have some sort of contract for that and you will accept responsibility for checking and acceptance on delivery but we will require 80 per cent payment up front . . .'
>
> 'Excuse me, may I just stop you for a moment. Sorry to interrupt, but you said that you would let us have final designs by Thursday and . . .oh . . . I see. Sorry. Yes, do go on . . .'

As long as you are thorough in keeping notes of the proceedings and go back methodically over the points that have been raised, there is rarely any danger in allowing the other side to proceed with their position statement. In the example above, for instance, you might well have decided by the end of the other side's exposition of their position that there is no way you would wish to do business with such people. Alternatively, you pursue some of the key matters first to decide whether there is the possibility of a deal.

> 'Thank you for setting that out for us. Perhaps I might just take one or two of the points you have made and look at them. We have no difficulty over subcontracting as you retain the contractual obligation on quality and suitability and, of course, for receiving and checking prior to our acceptance. Before I move on, has there been any misunderstanding over those points?'

It is not difficult to identify what advice might be given as to how to handle interruptions made when you are in full flow yourself. Should you ignore or override the interruption or accept it? Clearly the answer must be to accept it, ensuring that you know precisely where you were in setting out your case so that you can readily return to it later. Always allow the other side's case to be as exposed as much as possible before you decide how to deal with it.

Men, you are all marksmen – don't one of you fire until you see the whites of their eyes.

Israel Putnam, *History of the Siege of Boston.*

9

Tricks and countering them

Confound their politics,
Frustrate their knavish tricks.

Henry Carey, *God Save The King*.

In negotiating, there are three categories into which all of the tricks that might be played can be put. These are:

O definitely dirty or dishonest tricks;

O reasonably honest tricks;

O quite acceptable tricks.

But, as with so many things to do with negotiation, different people will take different views of what is honest and what is either dishonest or on the borderline. In many cases, although a technique might be basically honest, it might be applied in a way which would be construed widely as dishonest.

It is always worrying to hear negotiators boasting about the tricks they pulled on their opponents since this implies that they have missed the point of what they were trying to achieve from the negotiation. Such attitudes indicate that there was no attempt to develop any goodwill and that the whole purpose of the negotiation about which they are boasting was to do a once-off deal and get as much as they could from it. They will always have to find a stream of new opponents since nobody is likely to come back for further treatment!

The use of dishonest tricks, or of otherwise honest methods but applied in a dishonest way, is a clear indication to most negotiators that they should not continue to deal with the trickster. If they do, they deserve all of the problems and subsequent difficulties they get.

There are actually many hundreds of different tricks in the negotiator's portfolio and only a small but representative sample will be dealt with here. They are, however, the more common tricks and many others are but variations on one of these themes. All negotiators should understand how to recognise that tricks are being played against them, should know how to counter them and when things have moved to the point where they should simply withdraw from any further dealings with that particular player of tricks.

DEFINITELY DIRTY TRICKS

But man, proud man,
Drest in a little brief authority,
Most ignorant of what he's most assur'd,
His glassy essence, like an angry ape,
Plays such fantastic tricks before high heaven,
As make the angels weep.

William Shakespeare, *Measure for Measure*.

Dirty tricks make no pretence to be honest at all. They are played by a negotiator who clearly knows that they are dishonest and are being used solely to gain advantage.

In spite of moves towards greater openness and partnerships in the buyer/seller relationship, there are plenty of occasions when dishonest tricks will be played to try to gain advantage. These, if they are spotted at the time, will undermine goodwill and make the tricked party very wary in future dealings. If they are not spotted until later, they will sour the continuing relationship and may even encourage the victim to find ways of recovering some of the advantage lost.

It should be noted that people and organisations that are given to dirty tricks are generally quite ruthless about them and will have more than one to play in any given circumstances. If you encounter one such device, beware of others for they are almost certainly in the pipeline. Even better, if you can avoid doing business with the people who are perpetrating them, do so. While you are dealing with them, you will never really know where you stand.

In this category, techniques over which there is unlikely to be argument – they are dishonest wherever they are applied – would be 'facts' that are not facts and some of the approaches described under the 'standard terms' heading.

201

REASONABLY HONEST TRICKS

Here we begin to cross the borderline where some will believe that the tricks are honest and others will feel that they are fair game. When considering the range of dirty tricks available, the common factor was that they were played by people who knew that they were not being honest in what they were attempting and were trying to gain advantage from unreasonable or unfair practices. Even with those dirty tricks, one could take the line that it is up to the negotiator to see them, react accordingly, use the necessary counter-plays and either withdraw from the negotiation or proceed with a degree of caution, ever on the lookout for the next dirty trick.

But with reasonably honest tricks, there would always be argument as to the integrity of the player and the gullibility of the victim. From the selection below, it is fair to consider the 'gazump' and the request for off the record information as reasonably honest, but a few of the other techniques might be brought into this category as well. There are no absolutes, but some tricks are more dirty than others.

QUITE ACCEPTABLE TRICKS

These would be considered as fair game in almost any environment where they were used. They are devices to open up areas of negotiation progressively, persuade your opponent to discuss matters which he may have been reluctant to consider, move things along at the speed you choose and probe hard into aspects of the other's case.

There would generally be little difficulty in agreeing that amongst the techniques that could be placed within the acceptable classification would be the good guy, bad guy scenario, killer questions and the Russian front.

FACTS WHICH ARE NOT

Information put forward during a negotiation to influence the other party may be factual or may be false. Where it is false, and the user knows it to be false, this is unquestionably a dishonest trick. Whenever facts are quoted in support of a negotiator's case, it is

wise to ensure that there is some way to ascertain their veracity. The more important to the case, the more important to check them. Where facts are quoted by honest negotiators, they will generally be able to give you routes by which you can check them as they have nothing at all to hide. But other 'facts' may not be so easy to check, particularly those given 'in confidence'.

> 'Look, I shouldn't be telling you this and my boss would kill me if he knew I had, but three of the biggest retailers are taking this line at present and branding it as their own. That just shows you the quality and value we are offering.'

> 'We have just installed two of these in Buckingham Palace but, of course, they won't let us say so officially.'

Another version of the dishonest fact is that where the negotiator believes the information to be correct and provides it in good faith.

The fact that the other party believes what is being said should not deflect the negotiator from pursuing the supporting data with just the same rigour as if he was thought to be providing misleading information deliberately. Where information is significant to your decision, it must be checked.

The Replacement Window Salesman

We had moved house and knew that many of the timber window frames were rotting and in need of replacement. We studied the market carefully and made a short list of those we found most attractive, which seemed to offer an appropriate range and about which friends and neighbours did not seem to have any horror stories. Salesmen were invited to call to measure up, explain the features of their range and prepare quotations.

In the first round, we saw off those who insisted on sitting in the kitchen and not budging until we had placed the order 'on the basis that you can cancel without any commitment within seven days' because that was just one not quite honest trick to which we took exception. We were then left with a list of three from which to choose. One of the salesmen explained that their windows were the only ones on the market to have BS5750 accreditation on seven different features, so that meant that they were truly the best quality on the market.

I asked if that was what holding such accreditation meant (knowing, of course, that it was not) and the salesman confirmed his view without a trace of doubt. I suggested that he should check what he was saying, but not from his sales manager, who had given him the information in the first place. Two days later he rang me to say that he had checked thoroughly and discovered that he had been wrong. The accreditation covered consistency of quality rather than absolute quality.

Having told him that we would not be buying his windows, but not for the quality reason, I enquired what he would do when talking to future prospects on the quality issue:

'I'm going to have to think about that one.'

THE SNOW JOB

This describes the instance where you are inundated with paper-work about a contract which you have to wade through to find those bits that are relevant. This may be caused by carelessness or sloppiness on the other party's part, or it might be a deliberate attempt to make you overlook some of the terms that your opponents do not want to have brought into the open. The technique is also used in litigation, where the arrival of truckloads of the other side's records three days before a trial is intended to put you at a severe disadvantage.

When this happens during a negotiation, it is not necessary to decide whether it was a deliberate trick, designed to confuse, or an accident of incompetence. Either way, you cannot do your job unless the other party has made an effort to sort out the wheat from the chaff as it applies to the deal you are doing. If your enquiry has been unspecific, however, you may be to blame, and reverting to the other party for clarification is an admission of this. Nevertheless, some loss of face may be preferable to missing key points within the terms of the deal.

The dishonest snow job is not difficult to counter, as long as you see it for what it is and act firmly.

> 'Hello, Miss Simpson, good. The truck arrived this morning with the typical contract terms that you have used in the past. We have sent it back. Perhaps you could go through it and extract those terms that you are proposing to use on this contract, collect them together into a sensibly sized document without any extraneous clauses and let us have them back. Our contracts committee meets on Tuesday 17th and has to have relevant papers by the previous Friday, so if you are able to have it here by then, it can be considered alongside the others that are in the running. Otherwise . . .'

THE BATTLE OF STANDARD TERMS

This can be both frustrating and fun. It works on the assumption that the last set of contract terms that was exchanged is the set that applies to the contract in force. It is in general a valid assumption, although there are exceptions.

After a deal is negotiated, including perhaps many quite detailed terms, it is confirmed carefully and with attention to detail and the confirmation is accompanied by a set of standard terms of contract – the other party's terms. Many may be quite different from those which you thought you had agreed and, indeed, the other team may not even have bothered to discuss many of them with you, leaving you with the belief that your terms would be acceptable. When you receive such a document, you respond to correct any of the terms that are not as you had expected and the lack of a response suggests that your view has been accepted. However, at another point in the correspondence which follows, their terms are inserted subtly once again. That is when it is easy to overlook their arrival because, when they are checked against the previous set that are on the file, they are found to be the same!

Where this approach is used deliberately and with careful timing, it has to be seen as a dishonest practice because it is certainly designed to mislead. It can be countered by administrative vigilance or by ensuring that the *actual* terms are agreed and signed off together with a statement that other terms will not supersede them unless clearly signed by both parties.

SUBJECT TO APPROVAL

This is another trick which can be played some time after a negotiation seems to be complete and vigilance may have dropped. The terms appear to have been negotiated satisfactorily and the two negotiators have parted with goodwill on both sides and moved on to their next tasks. One side confirms the terms but slips into the letter or standard form the expression 'subject to approval', probably with no indication of who has to approve what, why, or by when. Things proceed because nobody bothers to check just what it means and there is in any event the formal order to be placed. Some time later, when it is too late to open negotiations with another organisation, the true impact of 'subject to approval' becomes clear. Somebody on the other side has queried one or more of the terms and does not accept them. You now have a limited number of choices, always assuming that you do actually want the deal to proceed, namely:

○ threaten convincingly to cancel the deal;

○ accept their alternative terms;

○ reopen the discussion with an attempt to negotiate something better than the terms they now propose;

○ approach another company to try to do a similar deal with them at short notice;

○ argue (possibly in a quite dismissive way) that the time for 'approval' has long passed and that you are proceeding on the basis agreed.

Whichever route you select, you do need to bear in mind that the trick that has been played was underhand and deliberate. The other party is not likely to simply give in as soon as you object. You will have to be prepared to be very firm and not show any sign of weakness.

MISTAKES

Some mistakes occur through genuine oversight, while others may be made quite deliberately to gain advantage in a negotiation. They may arise at any time through to completion of a contract, for example:

○ when running through points of agreement during a negotiation, one or more points can be erroneously stated in the hope that the other side does not notice;

○ similarly, in summing up an agreement that is to be confirmed in writing;

○ when writing down the terms and deliberately changing something that was agreed and claiming it to have been a drafting error – or even a 'typist's error', which is a frequently used excuse;

○ in performing against the contract when some details of the delivery are not as defined but differences are put down to a mistake in the contract when both sides knew that the agreement was actually different.

In the first three cases, the mistake, if noticed, can be put right immediately or may be picked up subsequently if the intended victim has kept appropriate notes of the matters agreed and can refer back to them, rather than relying on memory and arguing about different people's recollections of the same events.

In the fourth case, the person who has deliberately perpetrated the mistake has created a situation that may well backfire. It is in the hands of the recipient of the goods or service to refuse to accept what is provided or to refuse to pay where things are different from the contract. Here the argument that we both knew that the real agreement was different need carry no weight at all. If, however, it is the recipient who argues that the actual expectation was different from the contract, then the supplier should either attempt to clarify the position or withdraw the goods or service.

'I'm not surprised that they have failed if you are applying those criteria. Don't you remember that we agreed that we would use your standard contract to save the time and cost of getting it changed, but that you would allow 4 per cent failure before rejecting the whole batch? I did explain that with this experimental run we could not be sure to get down any lower than that and you were very keen to go ahead anyway. There's just nothing I can do now.'

'I clearly recall the discussion and your difficulties in predicting how well they would turn out from the new process. My notes from our meetings do say all of that. But I also noted that we would take out the discount and extend your P549c order to give you the extra money to allow for the higher reject rate at the works and extra inspection before packing at your end. We have sorted out the first batch so that we can go into production and I will counter charge you with any extra cost. The next batch has to be sorted at your works and be within the contract – as we agreed.'

MY FINAL OFFER

The 'final offer' ploy is interesting because you have to decide whether it is valid or not. Has your adversary moved to the point where further movement truly is impossible, or is this just a trick to try to convince you that you are at the limit? Again, the counter to this – whether it is honest or not – is not difficult. If you have reached a point in the negotiation that represents a reasonable agreement from your viewpoint, giving you enough of your objectives, then perhaps you can accept the 'final offer'. If you have not reached the point where you can be satisfied, simply ignore the finality and continue to discuss the changes that you require to the other side's position. But never debate the use of the word 'final' or you have been drawn away from what you truly should be discussing to another issue, namely arguing why it should *not* be the final offer.

> 'OK, I can see that you really do want this car and I don't want to let you go away from here disappointed. I'm too nice a guy for that. Tell you what I'll do. I'll give you the extra £50 for your own car, put on the mud flaps you want, tax it for you at cost, fix the alarm so it works properly and knock off the odd £85 on the marked price. That's my final offer.'

> 'I'm only interested in the difference that I will have to pay. We have already agreed all of those things that you have gone through. If you will accept the £3550 I am offering, then we have a deal.'

OFF THE RECORD

Whether you are dealing with journalists or negotiating towards a deal, assume that nothing is off the record.

> 'I think we can see some light in this now. I do sense that your production director is a bit hard to please, though. Off the record, what sort of person is she? Why is she pushing the terms quite so hard?'

It is quite obvious that any information conveyed to the other side, whether openly, in confidence, off the record, or by accident will be treated in precisely the same way. If it is of use to them, they will make use of it.

Similarly, if someone offers you 'off-the-record' information, ask yourself why that is being done. Why not simply give you the information openly? Generally, the answer is that the person offering is trying to form a bond with you personally that will encourage you to develop and provide further off-the-record information about your own side. In this respect, the giving of off-the-record information is like concession swapping – I have given you something confidential, now you answer this question.

The position here, then, is very simple. Treat anything that you are told off the record precisely as you do any other information coming to you; never give any information off the record that you would not otherwise have given.

THREATS

Some threats may be honest and some dishonest. Clearly the dishonest sort will be personal threats or threats to make sure something goes really wrong for you. But these are rarely used in business negotiations of the sort we have been examining here. But some threats may be used and need to be countered. For example, a supplier may threaten to withdraw some other critical supplies if you do not do the deal he is seeking, or a purchaser may threaten to withdraw a company's name from a list of recognised suppliers. Strictly speaking, these come into the dishonest category because they represent a misuse of power and a distortion of normal trading patterns.

Of course, if the withdrawal from a supplier list is because no business has been done for a specified time and seems unlikely to be done, this is not dishonest but a reasonable practice. Then the threat is fair as it is based on sensible business judgement. Similarly, if the withdrawal of other supplies is reasonable because they were supplied originally only on the assumption of an increase in trade between the two companies, then that may also be a fair approach.

It may or may not be possible to counter unreasonable threats. It is first necessary to ascertain whether the person making the threat actually does have the power to carry it out. If not, it can be dealt with firmly and the threatened act be avoided without loss of face. If the person does have the necessary power, and there is no way around it, then the overall position has to be assessed and a view be taken as to whether the overall condition that is being threatened makes a difference to the deal that was being negotiated. One is then negotiating a new deal – the additional factor has to be taken into account and entirely new needs, wants and desires be developed.

DERISION

Who can refute a sneer?

Rev William Paley, *Moral Philosophy*.

The derision scenario is known alternatively as 'you'll have to do better than that'. This depends on reacting to an opponent's offer – perhaps a concession that is being suggested – as if it is quite unbelievable and absurd. This response is difficult to overcome.

However, there is an appropriate response, which falls very much in line with many of the other approaches that have been proposed when you are faced with a difficult opponent. Here again, the answer is to examine what has been thrown at you and question it so that the person who has raised the sneer has to justify it. Then, while justifying it, the arguments put forward can be dissected patiently, examined, passed back for analysis and disposed of. In fact, the most suitable response can be quite annoying to the originator of the sneer because it has not thrown you off track and you are seen to be terribly reasonable. But that should ensure that the technique is not used again and you can proceed with a more sensible discussion.

'Oh, come on. That's ridiculous. You've got to do better than that!'

'I had not seen it that way. Why do you say ridiculous? That is an unusually extreme word to use. In what way do you feel it to be ridiculous?'

'Well, I mean. You can't expect me to accept that, can you? Not really.'

'If we are to take this any further, you will have to do better than that. Which specific aspect are you unhappy with? What were you expecting?'

'Well, I mean to say . . . it's . . . well . . . I think . . .'

Rarely does the derision approach have a useful impact when used against a competent negotiator. Even if what was put forward did have an element of the extreme in it, the riposte to derision will throw the other party off balance and have quite the opposite effect from what was intended.

There is a useful lesson here. Never try this approach yourself unless you have something more up your sleeve and can then demonstrate that the offer put to you truly was ridiculous!

Construction bosses have offered to lift a year-long pay freeze in the industry with an average 1.2 per cent increase in workers' pay packets.

Union leaders are dismissing the offer as 'derisory' and will be looking for a 3 per cent pay rise during the next round of negotiations on May 18.

General union GMB national officer Allan Black said: 'It didn't take long to reject their derisory offer . . .'

Construction News, 28 April 1994.

THE GAZUMP

Gazump: to raise the price of property, etc., after accepting an offer from (a buyer) but before the contract has been signed. [Prob. Yiddish gezumph, to swindle.]

Chambers 20th Century Dictionary, new edition 1983.

Unfortunately, this is a term which has become part of the English language, primarily because gazumping has become part of the culture in selling property in boom markets. In relation to purchasing private houses, it means reverting to the original buyer to tell them that somebody else has made a higher offer but that, if they are willing to top it, the house would still be theirs. During the late 1980s this became very prominent as house prices were rising quickly and there was a considerably overheated demand.

How is gazumping to be countered by the unfortunate buyer whose offer had been accepted? The best option at first is to engage the vendor in conversation about the price, the market, the universe and anything. By working around the issue, you may find out some more background than you had before, can identify whether this is just a ruse to persuade you to pay more, whether there really is another buyer, and whether, once you have permitted one gazump to take place, another will follow it. It is worth indicating that you are unwilling or unable to go up on your offer, perhaps pursuing the line that you thought there was an agreement and that you are surprised that your vendor is going back on it. While unlikely to work first time, this may give you further information.

But the strongest line of these is to refuse to move on the price at the first instigation that a gazump exists. Then see how your vendor reacts and try to assess whether there really is another purchaser. If you conclude that there is and that you really will lose the property if you do not increase your offer, then you have to revert to your objectives and targets and see how the increased price fits in.

Of course, if you are the vendor, you do exactly the opposite. Whether you have another buyer or not, you have to appear as if you do. You have to show an iron nerve so that the prospect is convinced that the price has to go up and offers more. And if the sole buyer's offer is not increased, you must have prepared an escape route so that you can still sell at the originally agreed price. If you are a vendor in this scenario, you should also move this item to the section on dirty tricks, rather than the one on reasonably honest ones.

Gazumping does unfortunately occur in many other circumstances in the commercial world where people will try to change a condition that has been agreed by using the argument that somebody else is willing to offer better terms. There are many direct parallels in the house purchase example to negotiating for any other product, goods or services. The same approaches will be suitable and the same probing for information is required.

The most effective gazump comes when the other party is so far down the road towards the contract that it is difficult, and possibly expensive, for them to back out. On houses, this can occur a short time before contracts are due to be exchanged, when the purchasers will have to spend more on surveys, more on solicitors and may even lose their own purchasers. On commercial contracts, the gazump is most difficult for a purchaser who has committed his own resources on the basis of the contract that is expected to be signed.

PROGRESSIVE ADD-ONS

This can arise only where a negotiator has been too lax in agreeing all the relevant terms or did not know enough about the topic to identify all the issues that had to be covered. This is perhaps to be considered as a reasonably honest trick because no negotiator should be expected to hold the hand of his opposite number and help him to achieve his own objectives. If the negotiator is too ill prepared or ill informed to do the job properly, then that negotiator and the business which he represents should expect to drive a less advantageous bargain.

"And I expect Madam would like to select a few accessories? A steering wheel perhaps? Heater? Passenger seat?"

Progressive add-ons provide the smart negotiator with the opportunity to gain extra ground after the main negotiation has apparently been completed. The ill-prepared negotiator is sitting back and feeling that the deal was somewhat easier to handle than had been expected, all the advice from others about care in handling this particular opponent had been unnecessary, that training and skill had surmounted all possible problems from the other side and the various elements of the deal had been knitted together remarkably well. And then, the progressive add-ons.

214

> 'Well, that about ties it up. We have got through much quicker than I had expected but I think that reflects the approach we both took and the fact that we have both been open, honest and forward looking. I will drop you a line confirming the fixed price we have agreed and the specific tasks your people will be undertaking. Thank you for being so positive and helpful.'
>
> 'Yes, I am pleased that we have been able to move things along so well. To avoid lots of extra correspondence, perhaps you would indicate that the expenses will be charged at cost.'
>
> 'Oh, er, but, um . . . well, alright.'
>
> 'And any meetings you want us to attend we will invoice at our scale fees.'
>
> 'Oh, er, but, um, I hadn't thought . . . well, alright.'
>
> 'And we might just agree a set rate of, say, £1000 per week for secretarial and support.'
>
> 'Oh, er, but, um, I hadn't thought, look here . . . well, alright.'
>
> 'And you will print the contract documents from our masters.'
>
> 'Oh, er, but, um, I hadn't thought, look here, just a minute . . . well, alright.'
>
> 'And . . .'

The power in this approach is that the victim tends not to want to back away from the original deal and does not appreciate the significance of all of the extras that are being thrown into it. No single factor is enough to force withdrawal from the deal but, together, they may well do so. But the factors are rarely aggregated in the victim's mind – he is too concerned with trying to keep on top of all the extras that are being thrown at him.

But looking at this trick coldly, even the ill-prepared or careless negotiator has to see it for what it is. It is a try-on to find out how much can be gained on the back of an agreement that was incomplete. Your counterpart will keep pushing until stopped. The fact that it is a progressive add-on ploy may not become apparent until a few minutes into the conversation. Perhaps, for example, the addition of expenses is quite reasonable; perhaps even the attendance at meetings is quite reasonable; perhaps the secretarial support is quite reasonable – and therein lies the problem. All of the extra demands are likely to be quite reasonable in themselves, but added together they represent something that has ceased to be reasonable.

As the victim, this trick may be countered in one of two ways, but first you have to realise what is happening:

○ *The detailed appraisal.* Allow the other side to proceed to the end of the list of extras and keep a note of all of them – after all, you are quite keen to know what is up his sleeve. Then, when the list is complete, add everything together, asking for assessments of all of the magnitude of the extras quoted, and arrive at the true 'final' price being sought. Return to each of the issues in turn, including the basic figure that you had agreed earlier under the misapprehension that it was inclusive, and negotiate them. Do the same with non-financial add-ons as well. Put aside any thoughts that you had an agreement and must stick by it; the trick that has been pulled quite justifies you in going back on that and seeking to open even issues that you have agreed. Do not allow your own ideas of integrity to permit your opponent to gain through the adoption of lower standards. Finally, decide whether this is the deal you wanted and, if it is, proceed; if not see your opponent off the premises.

○ *The cut-off* – as soon as you do appreciate what they are up to, stop the conversation. Point out that you do not wish to hear any more, show that you have identified the trick and revert to the original deal *as an inclusive deal.* Then await the response. Your opponent is now on the defensive and will have to argue why the extras should be included, will have to justify the amounts and try to have them included. You can be as negative as you wish. You can reopen the original deal that was made and challenge that as well.

Those approaches are useful when the progressive add-on trick is played on you, but what if you decide to play it? How can you make sure it has the greatest likelihood of success?

○ First, only try the trick as obviously as this on someone who seems to be green enough to fall for it.

○ Second, do not pursue one extra after another; intersperse your extras with other topics related either to the issue in hand or to other matters of mutual interest.

○ Third, never be too specific about the extras at the time; simply run through a small number of topics and say that you will sort them out later in writing. Then spell them out in a letter which gives the impression that they were discussed.

○ Fourth, do not mention extras at all but ensure that the wording which defines your agreement leaves you the scope to add them on later:

Invoice to cover legal services in respect of . . .
Amounts as below:
 Fees as agreed and confirmed in our letter dated . . .
 Expenses (as schedule) . . .
 Attendance at meetings (as schedule) . . .
 Secretarial support (as schedule) . . .
 Etc.

THE BOMBSHELL

In military operations, you have the opportunity to assess the bomb which your enemies might fire at you and to have planned your defences accordingly. Unfortunately, the essence of the negotiating bombshell is that you really did not have any chance to see it coming. The other requirement for the successful bombshell is that the timing has to be exactly right – too soon and the intended target has the opportunity to manoeuvre around it, too late and the target has moved somewhere else.

There are a number of counter-plays to the bombshell technique and their success will depend upon how well the technique was used and how alert the target is to what has happened.

'Great. That sorts out the final details on this and there are no more technical issues to resolve. We will put all of it into writing and put the materials on order. Now, about timing, it will be about 12 weeks before we can start . . .'

'Whoa, stop right there. You knew this was urgent and I am not spending any more on temporary measures. Next week or nothing.'

> '. . . and, in addition, I am instructed to inform you that the two colours that you had specified are no longer produced in that model but we will substitute shades numbered g431 and k566 from our shade card . . .'
>
> '. . . you should, therefore, hold the order in abeyance until samples in the colours which you propose have been approved in writing by our project manager . . .'

> 'Yes, I can explain why it is more than that. The discount room rate applied only to rooms let to your team when the hotel was not full and we therefore had otherwise empty rooms. We have been full for the past week and turning people away so the full price has been charged. The arrangement is stated clearly in our booking terms.'
>
> 'I see. Since that was not explained when we agreed the discount and I have not been given a copy of your terms, I am not prepared to pay it.'

Some bombshells can arise through genuine misunderstandings: perhaps your deadline was not clear to the other party; perhaps certain terms were so self-evident to one of the negotiators that it was never considered possible that the other party did not know of them; perhaps the real importance of a seemingly unimportant detail was not understood.

Whether deliberate or inadvertent, the reaction should not be too rapid. Take a moment or two to examine the impact of the bombshell and to decide whether you would be within your rights to reject the new information or whether it can be made to fit your needs. Ultimately, you have to decide whether this final factor pushes you outside the range of acceptability that you had defined or leaves you with a deal which can still be accommodated. If it is outside, then it has to be rejected, or other terms have to be renegotiated. If it falls inside your acceptable range, it is still worthwhile attempting to reject it out of hand. Many bombshell attempts are not expected by their proponents to have a high degree of success, so when they are rejected strongly, they will be retracted by an approach that does not force the originator to lose standing as a negotiator.

'Oh, I am sorry about that. We should have ensured that the arrangement was clear. We will, of course, prepare another bill and cancel this one. But I am afraid that we will have to apply the house rule on discounts for your future bookings. I will give you the terms with the revised invoice.'

GOOD GUY, BAD GUY

After all of the examples of this technique being used by TV policemen, it is quite amazing that it has so much validity still to negotiating. But validity it does have. As with TV policemen, the requirement is that at least one of the negotiators facing you is quiet, reasonable, pleasant, seeking a mutually acceptable solution and a long-term relationship, while at least one other is aggressive, unpleasant, grasping and unreasonable. In its simplest form, you try to deal with the nicer person and to exclude the other as much as possible, failing to notice that you are influenced in what you agree with the nice negotiator by your reluctance to upset the other one.

Another version is to make it quite clear that the unpleasant negotiator will not be attending a certain session and that you would like to try to finalise certain of the terms there and then. The argument is not put specifically that it will be easier without the problems engendered by your difficult colleague, but that is inherent in the proposal. There is then pressure to reach agreement at that session, rather than leave the issues open until a future meeting which Mr Nasty will attend.

There are some who argue that the right way to handle this technique is to require the less pleasant of the two negotiators to step aside from the debate because his presence is disruptive or counterproductive. That, however, can be countered quite easily by the other side explaining that he is essential because he has knowledge or authority that the other negotiator does not have. A concession may be offered that the individual concerned will be spoken to about his attitude and told that he is being too aggressive. Since both the person doing the 'speaking to' and the person on the receiving end are likely to be fully aware of what is going on, this approach will simply reinforce the knowledge that the good guy, bad guy technique is working.

Too Nice a Girl

In one recent example which I came across, the nice person was a young, attractive woman who indicated by her demeanour that she disliked her colleague intensely and would gladly not work with him again. The negotiator whom she was against, a man, used various devices to talk only to her and she responded by agreeing to meetings which her colleague could not attend. Her opposite number felt the pressure to reach agreement with her, even to the point of pressing ahead much faster than was wise. In the end, the young woman did the deal on far better terms than she had a right to expect. Her rather too hasty opponent was somewhat annoyed to then hear from a third party that she had signed up at least three deals in the recent past by employing exactly the same trick!

The only sure approach to addressing this tactic and ensuring that it does not have an adverse effect on you or your team is to ensure that everyone on your side is fully aware of what is being used against you and is told not to lose the focus of the negotiation or to be influenced by it. Once this device has been brought into the open, it has remarkably little effect on negotiators, who are then able to study it and observe how it is being used, rather than be deflected by it.

Experience shows that the aggressive interruptions are generally less considered than the debate of the more reasonable members of the team. When they are made, they can usefully be addressed and analysed so that Mr Nasty has to respond in detail and justify his remarks. This will bring out any weaknesses in his arguments and put his worthwhile points on a par – but no more than on a par – with those of his colleagues.

Finally on this point, it is remarkable how often a Mr Nasty who has been well handled by the adversaries will not bother to turn up to future negotiating sessions.

THE SILLY OPENING

It is quite surprising how many people believe that the silly opening trick still has any impact. This requires you to make a first bid that is so absurd that everybody concerned knows that it is. The argument for entering such an offer is that you have given away nothing of your position but have then drawn your opponent into making a statement of his opening position. Since this opening bid will also be absurd, it is difficult to see what has been gained.

When used in local markets in developing countries, this pastime is popular with both traders and tourists alike. The traders see the tourists coming and play their first offer perhaps ten times as high as they would for a local person. The tourist states an apparently absurd low figure, both assess a number about half way between the two offers and the tourist eventually pays something not far above that. The local trader is quite happy – what is trade for if not for encouraging the free flow of money from those who have it to those who do not? And the tourist is quite happy, having just driven down the asking price for the item by perhaps 40 per cent, simply by being better educated, sharper witted and more worldly-wise than this simple local trader.

But, whilst great fun on holiday, is this really what serious, sensible commercial negotiation is about? Of course it is not. There used to be a belief that civil servants would each year submit applications for annual budgets that were twice what they truly needed, confident in the knowledge that all figures were halved as soon as they were received. Things have become more sophisticated than that nowadays – at least, they have in most places – but the overbidding scenario is still quite common.

In normal contract negotiations, the silly bid is quite damaging. It will be seen by the other party as absurd and will not help in the goodwill and relationship building process. Neither will it flush out useful information from the other side. They will counter with an equally silly offer. But that is only if they bother to respond at all. It has to be borne in mind that your silly opening may result in your bid being excluded without further discussion.

> 'We were hoping to have this work on the car park done by Taybal Construction but the initial price indicator they have given us is three times what we expected. I am therefore going to ask three firms on our selected list to give me formal bids for the work.'

> 'Yes, I do appreciate you have had nobody looking at your house. But I told you that it was overpriced – perhaps by as much as 30 per cent . . . well, no, a higher price does not necessarily attract the better quality buyer . . . well, no, I don't think it gives the impression that it is a superior property . . . well, no . . .'

> 'This is ridiculous. Do you know what they have come back with? They claim the extra work cost £32,000, and they demand an extension of time and the extra overheads. Ridiculous! We offered £850 so that we could flush out their arguments and a price to negotiate . . . but this . . . nonsense . . .'

Perhaps the main area where silly openings still prevail is in negotiations between employers and employee representatives over working and employment conditions. But even here, the evidence is of more realism, perhaps reflecting the reluctance of most of those involved to waste weeks simply to move through the nonsense element of the negotiation and arrive at the real meat of the discussion. In this respect, demands and offers do still tend to target solutions significantly outside the area that it is anticipated the other side will accept, but the opening extremes have moved closer together. Old habits die hard and the process is well understood by both sides.

> 'We'll do without all the pleasantries. We are here to sort this out, today. We have seen the profit figures and know what is due to our members. There has to be an overall increase of 15 per cent, one additional week's paid holiday, more into the profit sharing scheme, a 32-hour working week and a complete upgrading of all the welfare benefits and a reduction in dividends.'

> 'We certainly can sort it out today. No problem. I'll tell you right now that the board voted yesterday for a three-year freeze on all costs. And that includes everything you have just listed. Now, do you want to talk about the snooker tournament?'

Beware of those who preach the message of silly openings; there may still be instances in the commercial world where they have relevance but they are few and far between and you could do serious damage while searching for those rare cases. In any event, the careful selection of other techniques will produce at least as much benefit, while carrying significantly less risk of disaster.

THE RUSSIAN FRONT

There are two definitions of this technique prevalent amongst negotiating trainers, but one is more effective and significant than the other.

In the first definition, the Russian front is a threat:

'If we do not get this sorted out, then the impact on you will be . . . (to send you to the Russian front).'

This has been dealt with earlier under the section on threats, and no more needs to be added except to say that, in this form, it is rarely used but frequently written about.

The second definition refers more to Napoleon and reflects the fact that, during his advance on Moscow, the Russians simply let him advance more and more until his lines of supply were too weak and his troops exhausted. In negotiation terms, this involves drawing the enemy further and further in to your camp, letting him become more and more involved, perhaps more and more interested personally in the deal and the achievement of winning it, and thereby encouraging him to lose sight of what it was he set out to achieve.

In its simpler form, the Russian front technique can be used when someone from the other side seems to want to hold the stage and keep talking. By allowing this to happen, drawing him out so that he says more and more about his side of the deal, you will have won all that you were seeking without firing a shot.

This technique is unlikely to be effective on an experienced and capable negotiator (experience alone being inadequate) who will not be encouraged to say too much without response from the opponent and who will not become too deeply involved in the task that faces him.

THE DUTCH AUCTION

This is another technique that can be used openly and with honesty or in a more underhand and dishonest way. In principle, a number of people have bid for a contract and are then invited to outbid the others after being told just enough about their competitors' bids to encourage them to improve theirs. The approach in its purest form is generally frowned upon in the public sector because there is no means of ensuring that all bidders had equal opportunity to submit their best offers. However, even the public sector has identified that it is acceptable to seek offers, then discuss them with the bidders and perhaps give a gentle indication to each bidder as to how their bid stands with relation to the others, and then invite all or a selected group of bidders to submit their 'best and final offers'.

In some instances, it is quite common to find that a small select group of bidders has been called to see the buyer and will each have a turn. The turns rotate around the bidders until either there is only one left or the buyer can see that the best offer has been obtained. The contract is then placed with the winner from the Dutch auction.

The Dutch auction is a game of wits and courage. You must be totally clear about your objectives before you enter into it – whether as the buyer or the vendor – and seek to achieve just that. If at any time your objectives do not seem to be available then:

○ as the buyer, you have to take stock and decide whether any one of the suppliers is near enough to your needs to be awarded the contract – it is worth examining at the same time whether you have squeezed so tight that you will not be given the service you expect;

○ as the vendor, you should not allow yourself to be pushed beyond the baseline which you set yourself earlier in the negotiation – remember your needs and wants and either hit your target or withdraw.

The Arabian Dutch Auction

A colleague and I were called to a government department of an Arab country after we had put in a proposal for providing assistance on a major computerisation project. We were given a specific time and location and asked to be ready to make a presentation to a selection panel. When we arrived, the reception area was filled with teams from the other three candidates, all of whom had been given the same time. We each in turn were to be called to make our presentations, with some of us clearly waiting a very long time.

We smiled, relaxed, drank tea, chatted together about everything except anything to do with our work, and waited until we were called.

Eventually our turn came. We made our presentation, answered our questions, refused to give an immediate discount, and were asked to wait outside with the others. We discovered that one of the teams had left in bad spirits, clearly having been told they were not in the running. The rest of us waited while the client team, presumably, discussed which of us was to win.

It was becoming clear that we were about to be put through the old Dutch auction routine with each being asked in turn to knock off more and more until we dropped out – rather like a reverse game of poker where we lowered rather than raised the stakes.

We were called back last and, while we waited, had quietly agreed that, as we were last, we were likely to be the favoured firm. We decided not to give any discount at all as we had no idea about the pricing of the competitors or any of the other terms of their bids. We simply had no idea about the proximity of the competition and therefore no idea of the value of giving away a percentage. The client team was a little surprised and mentioned that both of the other suppliers had offered discounts and we were expected to do the same. We stood our ground, arguing that we had already given our 'best and final offer' so could go no better nor be more final.

Oh, yes, we did win the contract. And we discovered subsequently that the difference in pricing between us and the cheaper competitor was considerably greater than we would have wiped out by offering a discount. All we would have achieved with a discount was a smaller margin.

BRINKMANSHIP

The art of brinkmanship also requires nerves of steel but is possible only when there is a credible target date by which the negotiation has to be completed. This, of course, need not be real, only credible. Many examples of brinkmanship occur in politics and industrial relations. The US government definition of a deadline by which Russian missiles had to be removed from Cuba to avoid military action was one example, while there are many instances of annual wage negotiations being concluded on the day before workers are due to walk out of their workplaces.

In commercial negotiation, allowing a discussion to run up to a deadline is a way of forcing the other party to grant concessions that will allow you to do the deal.

'This has been rather more protracted than I had expected and I now have a problem. We programme the rolling mill on the third day of each month. If I cannot put your order in by next Tuesday, the whole delivery will have to be delayed by a month at least, and that depends on how long after that it can be confirmed and how many others are in front of you. I have made a provisional reservation for the next programme, but unless it is confirmed by Monday ...'

'The chairman will be visiting this branch in two weeks time. He takes a strong personal interest in the state of the order book. We are running 14 per cent behind our target and I am not going to have to tell him that. I want firm orders bringing in before then. Here are the sales targets that each of you will achieve ready for the visit.'

A last-minute deal resolved the 'Battle for Orly' between Britain and France yesterday shortly before Air UK was due to test its right to land at the Paris airport without French permission. An agreement between John MacGregor, the Minister of Transport, and Bernard Bosson, his French counterpart, averted a showdown billed by Andrew Gray, managing director of Air UK, as 'pistols at dawn'.

Julian Nundy and Mary Braid, *The Independent*, 16 May 1994.

KILLER QUESTIONS

'Is that negotiable?'

'Is that your final offer?'

This chapter on tricks will conclude on a topic that is not so much a trick as a powerful technique, as long as your counterpart does not see it coming and have an appropriate response ready. It must be included in the 'quite acceptable tricks' category.

The killer question aims to demolish the carefully constructed platform from which the opponent has been debating and place him at a severe disadvantage, forcing him to reveal far more of his hand than he had intended. In particular, it actually does aim to discover whether the point that is being challenged really is negotiable.

O *Killer question:*   'Is that negotiable?'

O *Feeble answer:*   'Well . . . I suppose . . . if . . . um . . .'

O *Good answer:*   'Just let me finish. I am also looking for . . .'

O *Good answer:*   'For what we have been discussing, I must achieve that.'

While the technique is quite powerful, it may be countered by ignoring the question completely or by a gentle denial that the issue is open to negotiation. The outright statement that the issue is certainly not negotiable may place you in a difficult position later when you do show a willingness to negotiate on that point. But even here, there are ways around the difficulty.

'You said categorically a few minutes ago that you would definitely not negotiate on the issue of taxing the expenses element.'

'Absolutely. But that was before you clarified what was included in your definition of expenses.'

There are many other killer questions that can be posed, but they have two features in common:

O first, the question has to be short, crisp and to the point, demanding an immediate and equally crisp answer;

O second, the target knows clearly that he is being asked whether the door is open on the issue concerned or closed.

By far the best approach when facing a killer question is not to answer it but to pursue another issue completely. By far the best approach when faced with this counter is to press on.

> 'Yes, I want to come to that later. But you did not answer my question as to whether those standard terms are negotiable. Are they?'

10

At the end of the day

RECOGNISING A CLOSE

Many of the failures to close a deal at the first opportunity are caused by inability to recognise that the 'closing range' has been reached. This in turn may be because neither of the protagonists had recognised that there was such a thing as a closing range.

"Should we go over this once more?"

Both parties will have set out with a view of their needs, wants and desires, and will have modified these as they went along – with very little if any modification of their needs, more to their wants and perhaps some movement in their perceptions of their desires. So both will now have a clear picture of the position they can expect to reach and whether that is within their acceptable limits – the closing range (see Figure 10.1). If it has become clear that the deal will not fall within that closing range, then they should have broken off the discussion long ago, or changed their approach so that the outcome was more likely to be acceptable.

The ability to see that terms within the closing range have been achieved, and that they are likely to satisfy the other party as well, can reduce the time taken to finalise a negotiation and avoid confusion during the process of closing the deal. One of the key skills of closing is to be able to identify just when agreement on any specific

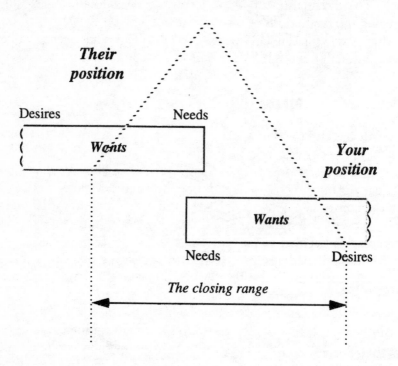

Figure 10.1 Targeting the closing range.

issue is within reach and then to grasp it and drive it home. The opportunities to do this will rarely be obvious; the adept negotiator has to see them when they are and make them when they are not.

A wise man will make more opportunities than he finds.

Francis Bacon, *Essays.*

The objective in commercial negotiation is rarely to squeeze out the last little drop as this will be seen as pedantic, greedy and petty by your opponent and, as with so many facets of the process, run counter to your aim of building relationships and goodwill. Furthermore, taking a considerable amount of time to debate very small issues is not cost-effective for either party. Simple, straightforward suggestions as to the final point of agreement on issues where the closing range has been found will speed the process of closing and make further business between the two of you appreciably more likely. The essential feature is to keep at least as good a balance in agreeing the final points as you have negotiated on the larger issues. In that way, you can be sure to achieve all of your wants while giving away just enough for the deal to be acceptable.

FINALISING THE DETAIL

Towards the end of a complex negotiation, no matter how carefully you have kept notes, no matter how carefully you have reviewed them between sessions, and no matter how carefully you have tried to clear up outstanding issues during successive sessions, you will have a number of loose ends outstanding as you draw near the close. Indeed, you may have left these loose ends quite deliberately: perhaps they seemed to be particularly sensitive points which you back-burnered; perhaps they seemed to be important at the time but their true significance has become clear as the whole deal has fallen into place; perhaps some represented matters which were dependent upon other larger issues being finalised.

All the best techniques for reaching agreement on these outstanding points build on the fact that there is by this time a mutual will to reach agreement and that the issues need to be handled gently but firmly. The important thing is that you retain the initiative in how the remaining points are handled. They may each in themselves

231

be small, but you could give away some quite significant gains made earlier if you are not alert.

Amongst the techniques that might be used, perhaps the most constructive and productive are as follows.

Presuming

By this technique you identify an area where agreement is still to be reached and simply presume an appropriate point at which you feel your opponent will agree. You then state it in a way that makes it seem clear and obvious that the matter can be closed there and then. When presuming, however, take it one step at a time. If you are greedy and presume too much at once, you may meet opposition. Approach this technique by nibbling, not by biting.

> 'Fine, that seems to have sorted out the key issues that we listed this morning. I am delighted that we have been able to reach agreement so quickly. I have a note here, though, about delivery. I take it that the small amount of non-containerised product will be palletised and wrapped and that you will send them on vehicles with hoists and pallet movers so that they can be placed exactly where our people need them on site.'
>
> 'Oh, well, we don't have that sort of truck ourselves. But we hire in anyway and can make sure we get the right sort. Yes, no problem.'

Paraphrasing

This consists of putting what you think was agreed, but which was not stated clearly, into a form of words that particularly suits you. In negotiation the technique enables you to achieve two different objectives, namely:

○ to clarify what has been agreed with a different form of words so that it is quite clear to both parties what was intended, but also

○ to place a slightly different emphasis or meaning on what has been agreed in outline previously.

Probing

This technique is useful when you are not sure what the other side might accept and wish to obtain further information prior to presuming. This, of course, is something that you have been doing throughout the negotiation process but it comes into its own again on points of detail at the end. The probe may also take the form of the simple enquiry as to what was in fact agreed on a particular issue, but it is essential to ensure that such an opening does not give your opponent the opportunity to make a significant gain out of your question.

'What method would you be using to get the palletised product right up to our workfaces?' .

'Oh, you would want it palletised at the workface. It would have to be wrapped to keep it secure – but we could do that quite easily. We would need to use vehicles with some sort of lowering and moving gear on them; you could leave that to me to sort out. I don't know about the cost, though.'

'Oh, please don't let us open up the cost issue again. What was it that we said about the markings on the crates? We did talk about part number and order number, if I recall.'

'That's right. I'm happy to put your order number on each crate but the part numbers would give us a problem. I cannot do that without a lot of extra effort.'

'Why would that be . . .?'

Prevarication

You should avoid this on your own part at the end and you should also be on the lookout for it from the others. Prevarication can arise for two principal reasons:

○ the belief that there is still something to be squeezed out of the deal;

○ uncertainty about certain of the terms negotiated.

If, alternatively, the person opposite you is inherently indecisive, that will have become obvious during the negotiation and should not be a revelation solely during the close. Prevarication has to be dealt with as matters progress either by:

○ agreeing each issue carefully in turn and confirming it so that there are never any large steps, simply a number of small ones; or

○ insisting that the prevaricating negotiator breaks off and returns later with a decision so that the next issues can be dealt with.

Where the opponent is prevaricating in order to draw more benefit out of the deal, that has to be dealt with firmly and issues should not be reopened for further debate where they have been agreed previously. If an attempt at prevarication is made on the basis of lack of clarity in what had been agreed, your notes and recollections should be put clearly and positively to avoid covering the same ground again, perhaps with a different conclusion.

> *Quoth Hudibras, I smell a rat;*
> *Ralpho, thou dost prevaricate.*
>
> Samuel Butler, *Hudibras.*

But prevarication arising from genuine doubt needs to be dealt with by taking the doubter through the agreed features and ticking them off one at a time in order to identify which of the points gives rise to the concern. These can be reviewed and confirmed with the necessary positive messages being given about each.

MAKING THE CLOSE

The great majority of closes will not require finalisation of all of the detail that has been discussed during the negotiation. Most will have been agreed as things progressed. On complex deals, it is important to both parties to close certain issues as they go along. This applies particularly to the principal issues which will determine whether the overall deal is done or not. If the headline matters cannot be agreed, then there is no point moving on to the more detailed topics – they will have too small an impact on the overall position to be the main drivers upon which the ultimate decision and agreement is based.

The close therefore requires you to ensure that the headline issues which were agreed were clear and appropriate and then to finalise and agree the lesser issues. One of the advantages of summarising around the key issues is that it identifies to both parties the size and significance of those features as against the minor details. This makes the smaller issues easier to agree. It will be clear from this that you should ensure that you do the summing up yourself and do not leave it to the other side. You should choose the appropriate moment, the sequence in which the summary is presented and, if necessary, put your own interpretations on uncertain issues during the summarisation.

Beware, however, of the jump to close, simply because you wish to retain the initiative. When the headline issues have been dealt with, or largely so, it is too easy to sweep away the others as of little relevance and either not deal with them at all or assume that they will be sorted out by somebody else at a later date. There is certainly no harm in deferring points for later negotiation but, where that is done, it should be a clear and conscious decision rather than an act of carelessness. The jump to close may be your choice because:

○ you do not wish to handle the detail;
○ you wish to be seen as having achieved a good deal quickly;
○ there was a deadline to be met;
○ you did not have a grasp of some of the issues and felt it better for them to be dealt with by others.

Alternatively, you may have been pressed into a jump to close by your opponent, who would much prefer to have the headline issues agreed but not the detailed points, on which he may feel he can gain much by leaving them unspecified.

The question of deadlines has been examined under the heading of tricks and the various techniques and counters need not be examined again here. It is at the close when deadlines become important and when the newly announced deadline can be most difficult to handle. If a deadline is known at the start of the negotiation, events can be planned and their progress monitored against that deadline but, when such a target is pulled out of the hat at the last moment, it is more difficult to deal with. Even a hat-pulling trick that you play yourself can put unnecessary and counter-productive pressures on your own side, perhaps even more pressure than that put on the opposition. Deadlines that are not genuine and essential are to be avoided during the closing stages.

CONFIRMING THE DEAL

It is quite amazing how many deals which have been carefully and fully negotiated are then fouled up by careless or incomplete confirmation. So much of the preparation, the face-to-face debate, the concession swapping and the detailed consideration given to points during the close can be lost because the interest has gone out of the contest once the terms have been agreed. It is for the negotiator to ensure that all of the work that has been done is confirmed and fully and correctly documented. While the task can be handed over to others, the checking and final approval has to lie in the hands of the negotiator in order that the understandings reached during the discussion are reflected fully and accurately in the subsequent contract.

There will, of course, be occasions when the terms can be recorded adequately by the negotiator so that the documented details can then be transcribed into a contract by others and, as long as there are no additional issues to be dealt with, that will be a satisfactory approach.

"That wraps it up, I'm sure Mr Sinclair has got all the details down"

Because there are often issues which were not totally agreed, even by the efficient and fully effective negotiator, the person confirming the terms of the deal may be at an advantage. This is the point at which further presumptions might be made, your own specific terms and conditions of contract be imposed, or your own interpretations of uncertain issues be claimed. None of this is unfair or unreasonable – the other side has the opportunity to refute anything you put forward and any such issues should represent only marginal effects on the main deal anyway. Such marginal gains are worth having – especially if the alternative is that the other side place their own interpretation on them to your marginal disadvantage.

'Scrambled eggs' is the term often used to describe what can happen to an otherwise successful negotiation where the impact is spoiled by casual and careless confirmation. When the negotiating parties have to meet again to sort out the meaning of the written confirmation, this scrambling of what had been a clear agreement will:

○ create doubt in the mind of the recipient about the true intentions of the writer and the real value of the deal that had been done;

○ give the recipient the opportunity to reopen negotiation on issues where they feel that they might be able to obtain somewhat more advantageous terms.

Again, it is for the negotiator to ensure that this is not allowed to occur.

ENDING ON A HIGH

Where a negotiation has been successful and both sides have achieved enough to make them feel it was all worthwhile, then it is not difficult to end on a high. The event can be publicised and celebrated and can lead to strengthening of relationships and a determination to deal again with that same organisation. It is worthwhile ensuring that successful negotiations do not simply slip away into the routines of paperwork and the detail of implementation but are recognised as achievements, perhaps by separating clearly the negotiation stage from the implementation by a formal contract signing.

On the other hand, where success has not been achieved and there has either been a complete breakdown or a contract has been awarded to another negotiating party, it is somewhat harder to end on a high. Nevertheless, where there is a genuine interest in seeking agreement with that party again, this should be emphasised and the good things that have been achieved be highlighted. This is but one means of ensuring the gradual development of business relationships with companies with whom you hope to trade in the future. Even the failed negotiation can contribute some value to both of the protagonists.

Behold, how good and joyful a thing it is, brethren,
to dwell together in unity!

Book of Common Prayer, Psalms cxxxiii, 1.

REVIEWING THE PROCESS

After carefully and successfully planning, executing and completing a negotiation, the maximum benefit can be derived by conducting a review of what was done and the reasons for success. Such a review need neither be lengthy nor particularly detailed, but it should develop learning points for all of those who have been involved and for others.

There are three ways in which benefit may be derived from a post-negotiation review. These are:

○ the internal (team) review;
○ the manager/supervisor review;
○ the training appraisal.

The internal review is appropriate whether a team or an individual conducted the negotiation. It involves going back over what was done from the very beginning of the process until the end and assessing what worked well and what did not, what contributed to the result, which techniques were productive and which were less successful, and so on. By this means, the team or the individual will have a better understanding of the whole process and will be even stronger next time.

The manager review may well cover the same ground – and may indeed be done in lieu of the team review – but should also aim to identify the specific learning processes that are appropriate for each of the people from the viewpoint of their personal development and progress through the organisation. This should not only probe the aspects that the team/individual will have identified as being good learning messages but also extract those points which the manager knows need to be developed. When this is done immediately after a negotiation has been completed, it is easier to recall the details and compare actions with optimum processes.

In training negotiators, the most convincing demonstrations of good practice are those which the trainees can relate to their sphere of understanding. These should be drawn from actual negotiations and developed for use in training, whether formal or informal. It may be that good aspects drawn from a number of instances can be blended together and a single consolidated case study be developed for training purposes. Again, the more quickly these good practice examples can be promulgated to more junior or less competent negotiators, the more impact they will have.

However the post-completion review is handled, there is likely to be value in having someone involved in the process who took no part whatsoever in the negotiation itself. The independent person should be knowledgeable about the commercial environment and negotiation processes and able to balance what is heard against good practice comparisons. This prevents those involved arguing that certain approaches and strategies were inherently inappropriate and requires them to give consideration to factors that they may not have taken into account at the time.

Lookers on many times see more than gamesters.

Francis Bacon, *Essays.*

However, this independent role clearly has to be played with tact as nothing is more annoying to a team that has just achieved something worthwhile after considerable effort than having an outsider turn up and tell them in a superior way how they could have done better!

The advantages to be gained from crisp but effective post-negotiation reviews are too often lost because those involved and their managers are too busy to put them in place and, in any event, often prefer to be off in search of new interests and challenges. However, the process can be very valuable for all those directly involved and for many who were on the periphery. The check list in Table 10.1 may help by focusing on the ten principal headings that should be addressed during a review and, within those, the 30 key questions that will provide the most value from the feedback. The final question should also be asked, as it must be of interest to all concerned.

Table 10.1 The reviewer's 10-point plan: the post-negotiation assessment

1. **Purpose:**
   — Did the key business managers understand it?
   — Did it fit clearly into the business needs?
   — Was the required relationship clearly known?

2. **People:**
   — Was the best person or team chosen for the task?
   — Had their training been suitable?
   — Were they appropriately supported and managed?

3. **Briefing:**
   — Did the negotiator/team understand the purpose?
   — Was the briefing sufficiently detailed?
   — Did the briefing constrain the negotiator unduly?

4. **Preparation:**
   — Was the preparation thorough?
   — Was adequate access given to data and people?
   — How cost effective was the effort put in?

5. **Opposition:**
   — Was enough effort made to identify them?
   — Were their likely strategies analysed effectively?
   — Were their business objectives analysed thoroughly?

6. **Strategy:**
   — Did we evaluate all the appropriate strategy options?
   — Was an appropriate strategy selected?
   — Did it function as expected?

7. **Metrics:**
   — Were appropriate metrics identified?
   — Were they developed and applied?
   — What effect did they have on the process and outcome?

8. **Tactics:**
   — Were they applied with sufficient flexibility?
   — Were the other side's tactics suitably countered?
   — Did our tactics generate overall advantage for us?

9. **Reassessments:**
   — Were our position and progress evaluated correctly?
   — Were our needs, wants and desires re-evaluated?
   — Did we change our approach and tactics suitably?

10. **Closing:**
    — Did we see the closing signals and send the right ones?
    — Was the negotiation closed to our best advantage?
    — Was confirmation professional and accurate?

And, finally, did we generate appropriate goodwill and build the right relationships?

11

The round up

He believed that 'The championship course should call for long and accurate tee shots, accurate iron play, precise handling of the short game, and finally, consistent putting. These abilities should be called for in a proportion that will not permit excellence in one department of the game to affect too large deficiencies in another'. The championship course should also ask the player from time to time to take risks, rewarding him if he is successful and punishing him if he is not; the reward should be in proportion to the size of the risk, and the punishment should reflect the extent of a failure to overcome it.

Bob Ferrier, *The World Atlas of Golf Courses*, Colour Library Books, 1991.

Indeed, so should the championship course for negotiators. All of the skills should be present in good measure, but some in greater measure than others, and the course should test them all to the full. The players who win on the greatest number of occasions will be those who have evaluated the risks and the opposition and have made suitable judgements in the circumstances.

Readers who follow golf books and magazines will recognise that such publications have a style which is all their own. They carry extensive articles, photographs and diagrams showing you how it is that the top tournament players do so well. The implication is that, if only you could do the same things, you too would be a top player. If only. Of course, the writers themselves do not have to be top players; they have to be able to play a bit and they must understand the rules and requirements of the game. But as writers, they have to be able to analyse what it is that the top pros do well and what it is that most other players do badly. Then they write about the differences and the readers gain by the writer's ability to set out the specific things that will help them improve and enjoy their game all the more.

This book has set out to be the negotiator's equivalent to the golfing magazine. Packed with tips, guidance, hints, tools and illustrations of both good and bad practice, it aims to help everyone go out and play better and enjoy themselves all the more. It is not possible in negotiation to define precisely how to do everything – and John Harvey-Jones's views quoted in Chapter 1 which relate to general management apply equally to negotiation – but there does need to be a toolkit available from which to choose. Rather like the golfer's bag of clubs – whatever the shot, choose the right club for it.

But golfing analogies should not permit understatement of the book's serious purpose. The aim throughout has been to assist readers to obtain a better deal for the organisations that they represent. We have seen that the negotiator should set out to achieve:

○ *all* of the needs;

○ *most* of the wants;

○ *some* of the desires.

So, quite unashamedly, the approach has been to help the reader to win more than would otherwise have been achieved. This quite certainly does not undermine any concept of partnerships in business, nor of building goodwill or long-term relationships. All of these things should be built on the back of good, hard-won deals and do not supplant the requirement to strike hard but fair bargains. That has been the theme throughout, and that is certainly the right theme for negotiators to live by, for they can certainly only continue to live as negotiators if they keep their objectives firmly in sight and always aim to achieve them by firm but fair methods.

Quidquid agas, prudenter agas, et respice finem.
(Whatever you do, do cautiously, and look to the end.)
Anonymous, *Gesta Romanorum.*

The art of negotiation starts with understanding yourself, particularly your strengths and weaknesses, and continues with appreciating the driving forces behind your opponents and the basis of their approach. It relies very heavily on preparation, on being fully ready with your own information and strategy as well as being prepared for whatever is thrown at you.

Qui desiderat pacem, prepaeret bellum.
(He who desires peace should prepare for war.)

Vegetius, De Re Mil.

But, after thorough preparation, success in negotiation relies on the ability to discuss the issues, to analyse and appraise and to develop with the opponent an understanding of the mutual advantages in the deal that is being pursued. The negotiator has also to be a competent salesperson; able to sell the ideas that enable the target desires to be achieved.

Very often persuasion is more effective than force.

Aesop, Fable of the North Wind and the Sun.

Perhaps critically on this question of the approach, attitudes and abilities of the negotiator is the issue of honesty and integrity. Many negotiators are quite happy to have tricked their way into a deal, having used a number of devious devices to arrive there. They miss one very important point – that party will not willingly deal with them again. Even if the lack of integrity is not obvious immediately, it will become so as time and the deal progress. And there is also the worrying prospect that any lack of integrity might begin to be obvious even before the deal is done, thus making the prospect of a mutually agreeable outcome unlikely in the extreme. The most successful commercial negotiators are trusted by their opponents and manage to remain credible no matter how hard a bargain they are driving.

Magna est veritas et praevalebit.
(Truth is great and shall prevail.)

Thomas Brooks, The Crown and Glory of Christianity.

Being trusted does not, however, mean being trusting. Until you have incontrovertible evidence that your adversary is honest, has integrity and will not be shooting at you from the arsenal of dirty tricks, it is unwise to trust too much. Build the relationship, develop the deal and be sure that the other negotiator has the authority to deliver it. Nothing is worse that concluding a deal only to have it overturned by someone on the other side who has more power or authority. And never allow yourself to get quite to the point where you totally trust the other side and expose your case fully to them. Agree progressively all that needs to be agreed and leave nothing unclear that needs to be clear. Maintain a safe, commercial distance and remember that you are trying to win for you and they are trying to win for themselves. Even when your opponents profess to have your interests first and foremost in their minds, accept their generosity with caution.

There's daggers in men's smiles.

William Shakespeare, *Macbeth*.

Finally, it is worth returning to the topic of enjoyment. At the outset, the point was made that those who do not enjoy the challenge and stimulation of negotiation should leave it to those who do. Lack of enjoyment will inflict itself on the negotiator who strikes poor deals, treats negotiation as just another routine or fails to get to grips with the interpersonal skills which are essential. Enjoyment arises from knowledge, understanding, hard-fought battles, defeating the tricks and achieving outcomes that are fair but truly to your advantage.

To suffer woes which Hope thinks infinite;
To forgive wrongs darker than death or night;
To defy Power, which seems omnipotent;
To love, and bear; to hope til Hope creates
From its own wreck the thing it contemplates;
Neither to change, nor falter, nor repent;
This, like the glory, Titan, is to be
Good, great and joyous, beautiful and free;
This is alone Life, Joy, Empire and Victory.

Percy Bysshe Shelley, *Prometheus Unbound*.

It's unwise to pay too much but it's unwise to pay too little. When you pay too much you lose a little money. That's all. When you pay too little you sometimes lose everything, because the thing you bought was incapable of doing the thing you bought it to do. The common law of business prohibits paying a little and getting a lot. It can't be done. If you deal with the lowest bidder it's well to add something for the risk you run. And if you do that, you will have enough to pay for something better.

John Ruskin, 1819 – 1900.

Appendix I

Case Study: Negotiating a contract for estate management

INTRODUCTION

This case study is based on real events. It is referred to in the main text of the book, where learning points are drawn and explained in appropriate contexts. The case study is set out in some detail here in order that the main text may flow continuously through the stages and activities which might be required during the preparation and execution of a negotiation. The content focuses on certain techniques involved in the monitoring and measurement of performance during negotiations. As the material has not appeared in other texts, it is valuable for it to be set out in full detail here.

The case study examines an organisation owning the property it uses, including a large number of buildings of different types and applications, substantial grounds and infrastructure such as drainage, car parking and roadways. The user/owner has examined a number of options for employing contractors rather than continuing to use its existing in-house labour force to undertake repairs, routine and emergency maintenance and minor improvements. These studies have shown that there would be significant benefits in having an external contractor undertake the work on the various sites.

They produced a work specification, quality specification and hourly rates schedule and sought a combination of a lump sum price for specified work, together with quoted costs for typical jobs and a schedule of hourly rates to cover unspecified work. In accordance with UK and European law, the existing workforce could either continue to be employed by the client organisation or, without any immediate changes to their current terms and conditions, be transferred to the new contractor.

Following a formal pre-qualification and tendering process, tenders from prospective contractors were received covering the next three years' work and, as each contractor had ideas about the best way of handling the work, the client decided to negotiate some changes and upgrading to the specifications prior to placing an order.

For the purpose of this example, it is convenient to make a small selection from the number of topics that the client felt should be negotiated. They cover:

1. a second site nearby;
2. transfer of employment of the present personnel;
3. the site manager role;
4. disputes resolution procedures;
5. use of the existing maintenance plant and equipment;
6. redundancies declared by the contractor;
7. apportionment of risks arising during the contract;
8. the duration of the contract.

DEVELOPING A NEGOTIATION PLANNING NETWORK

A network relies on having knowledge of which activities must be completed before others can start and which other activities can follow once one is completed. In the case study, for reasons which need not be examined in detail here, the client purchasing the service knew that, until the issue of transferring the existing staff to the contractor was resolved, nothing else should be discussed but that, when that was cleared up, he wished to address the questions of extending the contract to the second site and the matter of the contract duration. In addition, when the transfer had been negotiated, he wished to seek assurances from the contractor on limiting the scope for making redundancies after the contract was signed and in place.

Thus, it can be seen that no actions precede that of agreeing the transfer of staff (item 2 in the list above).

After agreeing this issue, he would be willing and able to discuss:

O the second site;

O contract duration;

O redundancies.

This structure can be rationalised into the form of a chart showing the prior and following activities in the form of a list. The table below shows this for the case in question.

Topic	Prior activities	Following activities
1. Including the second site in the contract	2	3, 5, 7
2. Transferring staff to the contractor	—	6
3. The role of the site manager	1, 6	—
4. Means of resolving contract disputes	2, 8	—
5. Contractor buying existing plant	1, 8	7
6. Redundancies declared by the contractor	2	3
7. Sharing future risks	1, 2, 5, 8	3
8. The contract duration	2	5

By examining those activities which have no predecessors it will be clear which have to form the beginning of the network; similarly by finding those which have no essential successors, the finish of the network can be found. These can be represented by short lines running from left to right which carry their appropriate activity label. It is then a matter of drawing in the remaining activities, using the same system but reflecting the restrictions given above in the table.

Once the network has been drawn it should be examined to ensure that it is logical, represents a suitable approach to your negotiation and has the potential for being argued successfully and sustained if the other party in the negotiation seeks a different sequence.

When the network is confirmed as correct it may be used to control the sequence of the negotiation, as a device for monitoring and reporting progress and as a means of arranging that resources are available and deadlines met. These elements are discussed in the main text.

This yields a network for this case that is shown in Figure A1.1

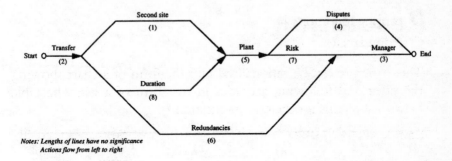

Notes: *Lengths of lines have no significance*
Actions flow from left to right

Figure A1.1 Activity planning sequence network.

Appendix 2

Centre for Dispute Resolution

The Centre (CEDR) is an independent organisation supported by industry and professional advisors to promote and encourage effective resolution of disputes. Mediation comes into its own when commercial negotiations have broken down and may be used before arbitration or litigation proceedings have been started or in parallel with them to try to achieve out-of-court settlements.

Mediation usually begins with the mediator having separate discussions with each party to obtain a briefing and to try to identify the true sticking points and possible areas of movement. The discussions are private and the parties can share confidences and reveal their true interests and objectives. The mediator thus has a unique view of both positions and the opportunity to identify, create and clarify possible solutions for the two parties to consider.

The mediator will from time to time seek the authority of one party to disclose certain previously private information where this is likely to lead to a solution which falls above the minimum needs of that party.

Agreeing to use the services of a mediator is not generally viewed as a weakness as, by that stage, it will be obvious to both parties that the negotiation is deadlocked and that mediation may be a way to identify a solution.

If the parties agree to mediate, any agreement reached with the help of the mediator can have whatever force – legal or otherwise – that the parties choose. The process is not evaluative but facilitative and the mediator does not therefore act as judge or arbitrator nor impose any solution on the parties.

Further information on the techniques and application of mediation, on the appointment of mediators and on how to obtain training to become a mediator may be obtained from:

Centre for Dispute Resolution
100 Fetter Lane
London EC4A 1DD
Telephone: 44 (0)171 430 1852
Fax: 44 (0)171 430 1846

Index